TARGET MATHS

Year 5

Stephen Pearce

Elmwood Press

First published 2002 by
Elmwood Press
80 Attimore Road
Welwyn Garden City
Herts. AL8 6LP
Tel. 01707 333232

Reprinted 2002, 2003, 2004, 2005, 2006, 2007, 2008, 2009, 2011, 2012, 2013

British Library Cataloguing in Publication Data

Pearce, Stephen

    1. Mathematics—1961–
    I. Title

    ISBN 978 1 902 214 238

Numerical answers are published in a separate book

Typeset and illustrated by Tech-Set Ltd., Gateshead, Tyne and Wear
Printed and bound by Bookwell.

PREFACE

Target Maths has been written for pupils in Year 5 and their teachers.

The intention of the book is to provide teachers with material to teach *all* the NNS objectives, as set out in the yearly teaching programme, and with *all* the children in their class able to work at their appropriate level of ability.

One of the key principles for the approach to teaching recommended by the NNS is 'controlled differentiation, with all pupils engaged in mathematics related to a common theme.' **Target Maths** is structured so that controlled differentiation is built into every lesson. How a teacher decides to use the material would depend upon the children's familiarity with the topic and the amount of time that is available.

Each lesson in the book is divided into four sections. The four sections are:

- The introduction: a clearly stated learning intention and, where necessary, explanations and examples of new work.
- Section A: activities based upon the NNS expected learning outcomes for Year 4 pupils. This section can be used to remind children of work previously covered, as well as providing material for the less confident child.
- Section B: activities based upon the NNS expected learning outcomes for Year 5 pupils. Most children should be able to work successfully at this level.
- Section C: activities based upon the NNS expected learning outcomes for Year 6 pupils. This section provides extension material for the faster workers and for those who need to be moved quickly onto more challenging tasks. Problems in Section C can also provide useful material for discussion in the plenary session.

The correspondence of the three sections to the NNS learning outcomes expected of different year groups provides a simple, manageable framework for both the formal and informal assessment of children's progress. The expectations in the yearly teaching programmes correspond to these National Curriculum levels.

- Section A   Year 4   consolidation of level 3, start on level 4
- Section B   Year 5   revision of level 3, but mainly level 4
- Section C   Year 6   consolidation of level 4, start on level 5

Both the NNS Teaching Programme for Year 5 and the Term Framework are in the Answer Book with **Target Maths** page references for all the NNS objectives.

The author is indebted to many colleagues who have assisted him in this work. He is particularly grateful to David Rayner and Sharon Granville for their invaluable advice and support.

CONTENTS

2

On these pages you will learn:

- **that numbers are made up from digits.**
  There are ten digits, 0 1 2 3 4 5 6 7 8 and 9.
  347 is a three-digit number, 3472 is a four-digit number, and so on.

- **to read and write whole numbers.**
  The way we read a digit depends upon its place in the number.

  2748 is two thousand seven hundred and forty-eight
  27 485 is twenty-seven thousand four hundred and eighty-five
  274 856 is two hundred and seventy four thousand eight hundred and fifty-six
  2 748 563 is two million seven hundred and forty-eight thousand five hundred and sixty-three

  TAKE CARE when a number has noughts in it.

  3006 is read as three thousand and six.
  600 502 is read as six hundred thousand five hundred and two

A

These figures show the distances between London and other cities around the world.
Write each distance in words.

1	Rome	1431 km	**6**	Cairo	3508 km
2	Chicago	6356 km	**7**	Lagos	5017 km
3	Beijing	8138 km	**8**	Singapore	10 852 km
4	Copenhagen	952 km	**9**	Berlin	928 km
5	Mexico City	8936 km	**10**	Caracas	7507 km

11 Copy the table, writing each distance in figures.

City	Distance to London (kilometres)
New York	five thousand five hundred and seventy-two
Moscow	two thousand four hundred and ninety-eight
Paris	three hundred and forty-two
Los Angeles	eight thousand seven hundred and fifty-eight
Johannesburg	nine thousand and seventy-one
Bombay	seven thousand one hundred and ninety
Rio de Janeiro	nine thousand two hundred and ninety-nine
Buenos Aires	eleven thousand one hundred and thirty-one
Calcutta	seven thousand nine hundred and sixty-one
Toronto	five thousand seven hundred and four

B

1 The table shows the areas of the largest seas and oceans in the world. Copy the table, writing each area in figures.

Seas	Area (square miles)
Pacific Ocean	sixty-four million one hundred and ninety thousand
Atlantic Ocean	thirty-three million four hundred and twenty thousand
Indian Ocean	twenty-eight million three hundred and fifty thousand
Arctic Ocean	five million one hundred and ten thousand
South China Sea	one million one hundred and forty-eight thousand
Caribbean Sea	one million and sixty-three thousand
Mediterranean Sea	nine hundred and sixty-six thousand five hundred
Baring Sea	eight hundred and seventy-five thousand seven hundred
Gulf of Mexico	five hundred and ninety-five thousand eight hundred
Sea of Okhotsk	five hundred and eighty-nine thousand eight hundred

The same areas are written here in square kilometres.
Write each area in words.

2 Pacific Ocean   166 240 000 km²

3 Atlantic Ocean   86 560 000 km²

4 Indian Ocean   73 430 000 km²

5 Arctic Ocean   13 230 000 km²

6 South China Sea   2 974 000 km²

7 Caribbean Sea   2 753 000 km²

8 Mediterranean Sea   2 503 000 km²

9 Baring Sea   2 268 180 km²

10 Gulf of Mexico   1 542 985 km²

11 Sea of Okhotsk   1 527 570 km²

C

The following figures show the populations of some European capital cities.
Write each population in words.

1 London   7 007 091

2 Brussels   953 175

3 Berlin   3 472 009

4 Budapest   2 002 121

5 Luxembourg   77 400

6 Vienna   1 806 737

7 Paris   9 319 367

8 Cardiff   302 747

9 Monaco   27 063

10 Rome   2 693 383

11 Athens   3 072 922

12 Sarajevo   529 021

13 Make as many five-digit numbers with a value of less than 26 000 as you can using these digits only.

Write each number in words and figures.

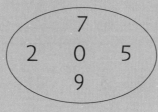

PLACE VALUE OF DIGITS

On this page you will learn to know what each digit in a number represents.

The value of a digit depends upon its position in the number.

Example   1 423 698

M	HTh	TTh	Th	H	T	U
1	4	2	3	6	9	8

The 1 has a value of 1 000 000.
The 4 has a value of 400 000.
The 2 has a value of 20 000.
The 3 has a value of 3 000.
The 6 has a value of 600.
The 9 has a value of 90.
The 8 has a value of 8.

A

Copy and complete by writing the missing number in the box.

1 369 = ☐ + 60 + 9

2 1426 = 1000 + 400 + ☐ + 6

3 2193 = 2000 + 100 + 90 + ☐

4 4537 = ☐ + 500 + 30 + 7

5 3858 = 3000 + ☐ + 50 + ☐

6 672 = ☐ + ☐ + 2

7 5724 = ☐ + 700 + ☐ + 4

8 2917 = 2000 + ☐ + ☐ + 7

9 1946 = ☐ + 900 + 40 + ☐

10 1156 = 1000 + ☐ + ☐ + ☐

11 8538 = ☐ + ☐ + ☐ + ☐

12 3532 = ☐ + ☐ + ☐ + ☐

B

Write down the value of the digit underlined.

1 39̲82

2 6715̲

3 24̲360

4 38 6̲74

5 185̲ 037

6 241 4̲26

7 1 6̲59 249

8 1 51̲8 598

9 3̲ 460 103

10 9 772 851̲

11 2 39̲6 910

12 3 8̲24 672

13 753̲ 217

14 4 805 2̲46

15 5̲ 130 909

Add 4000 to:	Add 30 000 to:	Take 200 from:	Take 100 000 from:
16 13 672	**19** 243 497	**22** 424 357	**25** 432 176
17 100 813	**20** 813	**23** 1 173 884	**26** 1 918 534
18 145 628.	**21** 1 545 628.	**24** 12 916.	**27** 6 259 019.

C

Write the answers only

1 317 496 + 60 000

2 1 854 031 + 9000

3 2 007 193 − 4000

4 62 584 − 20 000

5 450 267 + 700 000

6 3 194 805 − 2 000 000

7 7 436 + 1 000 000

8 5 219 320 − 4000

9 1 329 754 − 300 000

Add 600 000 to:		Take 7000 from:	
10 1 587 362	**12** 8174	**14** 28 298	**16** 1 211 471
11 204 189	**13** 5.	**15** 142 165	**17** 95 362.

On this page you will learn to multiply and divide whole numbers by 10 and 100.

Examples

×10	digits move 1 place to the left	$624 \times 10 = 6240$
×100	digits move 2 places to the left	$624 \times 100 = 62\,400$
÷10	digits move 1 place to the right	$4300 \div 10 = 430$
÷100	digits move 2 places to the right	$4300 \div 100 = 43$

A

Multiply by 10.

1	30	**9**	932
2	187	**10**	208
3	620	**11**	423
4	714	**12**	380
5	593	**13**	66
6	58	**14**	705
7	377	**15**	541
8	400	**16**	420

Divide by 10.

17	860	**25**	6000
18	90	**26**	3920
19	3000	**27**	3610
20	1530	**28**	240
21	700	**29**	7300
22	5400	**30**	2830
23	1670	**31**	4580
24	400	**32**	5000

Copy and complete.

33 $\square \times 10 = 8600$

34 $\square \div 10 = 62$

35 $\square \times 10 = 1390$

36 $\square \div 10 = 580$

37 $\square \times 10 = 2010$

38 $\square \div 10 = 417$

B

Write the answers only.

1 987×10

2 $1700 \div 10$

3 860×100

4 $1400 \div 100$

5 26×100

6 $2030 \div 10$

7 8000×10

8 $23\,000 \div 100$

9 $90\,000 \div 10$

10 2100×10

11 2400×100

12 $82\,100 \div 100$

Copy and complete.

13 $\square \times 10 = 7830$

14 $\square \times 100 = 82\,000$

15 $\square \div 10 = 380$

16 $\square \div 100 = 1300$

17 $\square \times 10 = 16\,420$

18 $\square \times 100 = 9400$

19 $\square \div 10 = 62\,000$

20 $\square \div 100 = 480$

21 $\square \times 10 = 43\,000$

22 $\square \div 10 = 2232$

23 $\square \times 100 = 350\,000$

24 $\square \div 100 = 20\,000$

C

×100	×1000

1	148	**5**	460
2	2430	**6**	3000
3	12 000	**7**	1800
4	700	**8**	90

÷100	÷1000

9	6000	**13**	80 000
10	197 000	**14**	600 000
11	1 000 000	**15**	4 000 000
12	2 360 000	**16**	1 709 000

27 540	5900

17	×10	**21**	×100
18	×1000	**22**	÷100
19	×100	**23**	×1000
20	÷10	**24**	÷10

123 000	2000

25	÷10	**29**	×100
26	÷100	**30**	÷1000
27	×10	**31**	÷10
28	÷1000	**32**	×1000

33 There are 14 sweets in each packet. There are 100 packets in each box. How many sweets are there in 100 boxes?

On these pages you will learn:

- **to use the symbols < > and =.**
  > means 'is greater than'.
  < means 'is less than'.
  = means 'is equal to'.

- **to work out the number lying half way between two other numbers.**

Example

Find the number half way between 36 200 and 37 800.

a) Find the difference between the numbers.
$$37\,800 - 36\,200 = 1600$$

b) Work out half the difference.
$$1600 \div 2 = 800$$

c) Add half the difference to the lower number.
$$36\,200 + 800 = 37\,000$$

- **to order a set of numbers in order of size.**

Example

Arrange 2581 2158 21 158 in ascending order.

Look at the highest value digits first.

2581	2158	21 158
↓	↓	↓
2000	2000	20 000

If the highest value digits are the same look at the second digits.

2581	2158
↓	↓
500	100

Therefore the order is 2158 2581 21 158.

A

Copy and complete by putting >, < or = in each box.

1 $7 \times 4 \;\square\; 40 - 12$ **7** $8 \times 5 \;\square\; 22 + 19$

2 $8 \times 3 \;\square\; 13 + 9$ **8** $3 \times 7 \;\square\; 35 - 14$

3 $9 \times 4 \;\square\; 49 - 11$ **9** $6 \times 4 \;\square\; 14 + 9$

4 $6 \times 3 \;\square\; 30 - 15$ **10** $9 \times 3 \;\square\; 16 + 11$

5 $9 \times 5 \;\square\; 25 + 21$ **11** $3 \times 6 \;\square\; 25 - 8$

6 $4 \times 8 \;\square\; 50 - 18$ **12** $5 \times 9 \;\square\; 31 + 16$

Put these sets of numbers in order, starting with the smallest.

13 863   2836   683   2386

14 5419   1945   5914   5149

15 2743   3472   3247   3274

16 1638   1386   1863   1836

17 4785   4758   4578   4857

18 6213   6312   6321   6231

Find the number that is half way on each of these number lines.

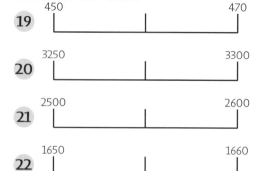

19 450   470

20 3250   3300

21 2500   2600

22 1650   1660

Copy and complete by writing a number in the box.

23 $240 < \square < 245$

24 $995 < \square < 1000$

25 $4120 < \square < 4150$

26 $3000 > \square > 2990$

B

Copy and complete by putting >, < or = in each box.

1 8 × 6 ☐ 24 + 25
2 6 × 7 ☐ 23 + 19
3 8 × 8 ☐ 32 + 33
4 9 × 9 ☐ 52 + 29
5 7 × 6 ☐ 80 − 37
6 6 × 9 ☐ 84 − 31
7 9 × 8 ☐ 100 − 27
8 7 × 7 ☐ 27 + 22
9 9 × 6 ☐ 27 + 26
10 8 × 7 ☐ 28 + 28
11 7 × 9 ☐ 100 − 36
12 6 × 8 ☐ 28 + 19

Put these numbers in ascending order.

13 4738   3874   3478   4837
14 52 287   52 783   53 872   53 827
15 19 162   19 612   19 261   19 216
16 16 006   10 606   16 060   10 660
17 14 231   14 321   14 421   14 312
18 30 003   30 030   30 303   30 033

Find the number that is half way on each of these number lines.

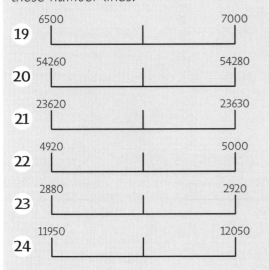

19 6500 ——|—— 7000
20 54260 ——|—— 54280
21 23620 ——|—— 23630
22 4920 ——|—— 5000
23 2880 ——|—— 2920
24 11950 ——|—— 12050

C

Copy and complete by putting >, < or = in each box.

1 150 ÷ 3 ☐ 7 × 7
2 72 ÷ 9 ☐ 64 ÷ 8
3 2·5 × 3 ☐ 15 ÷ 2
4 36 ÷ 9 ☐ 40 ÷ 8
5 15 × 7 ☐ 10^2
6 180 ÷ 30 ☐ 56 ÷ 8
7 0·5 × 4 ☐ 6·3 ÷ 3
8 36 × 2 ☐ 24 × 3
9 72 ÷ 8 ☐ 150 ÷ 15
10 54 ÷ 6 ☐ 3^2
11 14 × 5 ☐ 7·2 × 10
12 400 ÷ 5 ☐ 13 × 6

13

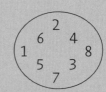

Use these digits once each. Make two different 4-digit numbers which give:
a) the largest possible total.
b) the smallest possible total.
c) the largest possible difference.
d) the smallest possible difference.

Work out the number that is halfway between these numbers.

14 3400 ←——→ 4400
15 19 300 ←——→ 20 000
16 25 280 ←——→ 25 380
17 17 400 ←——→ 18 200
18 16 680 ←——→ 16 740
19 6940 ←——→ 7020
20 32 900 ←——→ 33 400

On this page you will learn to make and justify estimates.

A

Estimate the numbers shown by the arrows.

1

2

3

4

5

6

7 Which snake is:
  a) half as long as Sally?
  b) twice as long as Sylvia?
  c) one and a half times the length of Cecil?

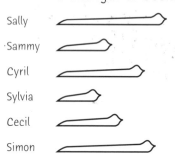

8 Sally is one metre long. Estimate the lengths of the other snakes.

B

Estimate the numbers shown by the arrows.

1 100 ↓ ↓ 200

2 90 ↓ 110

3 −10 ↓ ↓ 0

4 0 ↓ ↓ 100

5 40 ↓ ↓ 80

6 Six friends bought drinks. Five minutes later their drinks looked like this.

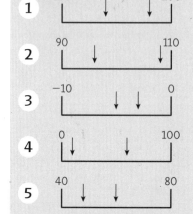

Jack   James   Joe

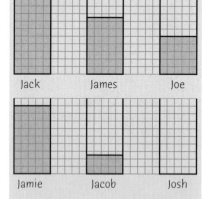

Jamie   Jacob   Josh

Who has drunk:
  a) three times as much as James?
  b) half as much as Joe?
  c) one tenth as much as Josh?

7 Jack has not touched his drink. Josh has finished his. Estimate the fraction left in the other four glasses.

C

Estimate the numbers shown by the arrows.

1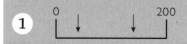

2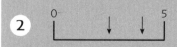

3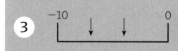

4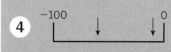

5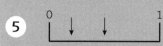

6 Estimate the number of 2p coins it would take to reach 100 m. The coins must be lying flat and touching the coins next to it in a straight line.

Explain your method. Use your method to make the same estimate for other coins.

7 Estimate how many sheets of A4 paper would be needed to cover:
  a) your table.
  b) the classroom door.
  c) the classroom floor.

On this page you will learn:

- **to round numbers to the nearest 10, 100 or 1000.**

Always look at the column to the right of that to which you are rounding.
If the number in that column is less than 5, round down.
If the number in that column is 5 or greater than 5, round up.

Examples

to the nearest 10	362	rounds to → 360	2137	rounds to → 2140
to the nearest 100	5941	→ 5900	8681	→ 8700
to the nearest 1000	6456	→ 6000	7568	→ 8000

- **to approximate calculations by rounding.**

Examples

$327 + 244 \rightarrow 330 + 240 \rightarrow 570$

$42 \times 9 \rightarrow 40 \times 9 \rightarrow 360$

A

Round these numbers to the nearest 10.

1	63	**7**	72
2	31	**8**	18
3	27	**9**	37
4	49	**10**	65
5	84	**11**	59
6	96	**12**	43

Round these numbers to the nearest 100.

13	836	**19**	461
14	194	**20**	727
15	505	**21**	283
16	343	**22**	852
17	299	**23**	418
18	654	**24**	970

B

Round to the nearest 10.

1	252	**4**	925
2	329	**5**	184
3	8	**6**	999

Round to the nearest 100.

7	476	**10**	2745
8	1632	**11**	3961
9	1050	**12**	253

Round to the nearest 1000.

13	6700	**16**	13 367
14	11 480	**17**	7812
15	15 620	**18**	9501

Approximate by rounding to the nearest 10.

19	$166 + 122$	**24**	$216 - 78$
20	$346 + 533$	**25**	38×5
21	$257 + 142$	**26**	72×6
22	$97 - 29$	**27**	49×8
23	$142 - 53$	**28**	96×7

C

Copy the sentences, rounding the number to the nearest 1000.

1 Lake Victoria has an area of 69 484 km².

2 The Polar diameter of the Earth is 12 714 km.

3 The car has a mileage of 73 521.

4 Jasmine won £2 319 278 on the Lottery.

Approximate by rounding to the nearest 10.

5	$267 + 142$
6	$272 - 64$
7	62×7
8	$683 + 279$
9	$498 - 317$
10	78×9
11	$435 + 183$
12	39×8

On these pages you will learn to recognise and order negative numbers.

Negative numbers below zero have a minus sign

Positive numbers above zero

−10 −9 −8 −7 −6 −5 −4 −3 −2 −1 0 1 2 3 4 5 6 7 8 9 10

We often use negative numbers with temperature.

Example

The temperature is 4°C. It falls 5°.

What is the new temperature?

Answer   −1°C.

A

Use the number line above.

1 Count on 4 from −3.

2 Count on 7 from −9.

3 Count on 8 from −5.

4 Count on 6 from −2.

5 Count back 7 from 4.

6 Count back 8 from −1.

7 Count back 12 from 6.

8 Count back 9 from 0.

Copy and complete by filling in the boxes.

9 −5 −4 ☐ ☐ ☐ 0 1

10 3 2 ☐ ☐ ☐ −2 −3

11 ☐ ☐ ☐ −6 −4 −2 0

12 −14 −10 ☐ −2 ☐ 6 ☐

13 −7 −5 ☐ −1 ☐ 3 ☐

14 5 3 1 −1 ☐ ☐ ☐

15 −6 −4 ☐ ☐ ☐ 4 6

16 −6 −7 ☐ ☐ ☐ −11 − 12

Look at the scale.

17 What temperatures are shown by the letters?

18 Which letter shows the coldest temperature?

19 What is the difference in temperature between:
   a) A and B   b) A and C   c) B and C?

20 What would the temperature be:
   a) if it was at A and fell 7°C?
   b) if it was at B and fell 10°C?
   c) if it was at C and rose 10°C?

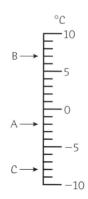

B

Copy and complete each number sequence.

1 −11 −9 −7 −5 ☐ ☐ ☐

2 −11 −8 −5 ☐ ☐ ☐ 7

3 −6 −4 ☐ ☐ ☐ 4 6

4 −14 −10 ☐ ☐ ☐ 6 10

5 5 3 1 ☐ ☐ ☐ −7

6 8 6 4 2 ☐ ☐ ☐

7 11 8 5 2 ☐ ☐ ☐

8 13 9 5 ☐ ☐ ☐ −11

Put each set of numbers in order, smallest first.

9 7 −3 −6 9 3 −1

10 9 −2 −8 1 4 0

11 1 −4 −7 6 −1 2

12 −2 0 5 3 −3 −6

Look at the scale.

13 What temperatures are shown by the letters?

14 Which letter shows the coldest temperature?

15 Give the difference in temperature between:
   a) A and B   b) A and C   c) B and C.

16 What would the temperature be:
   a) if it was at A and fell 14°C?
   b) if it was at B and rose 18°C?
   c) if it was at C and fell 17°C?

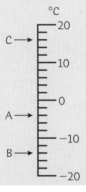

C

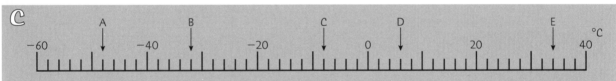

Look at the scale.

1 What temperatures are shown by the letters?

2 Give the difference in temperature between:
   a) C and D   c) C and E
   b) B and C   d) A and D.

3 What would the temperature be if it was:
   a) at A and rose 34°C?   c) at C and fell 26°C?
   b) at D and fell 18°C?   c) at B and rose 48°C?

Copy and complete the tables showing changes in temperature.

5

Old	Change	New
−4°C	+8°C	4°C
6°C	−11°C	
−23°C	+17°C	
12°C	−15°C	
−10°C	+9°C	
7°C	−20°C	

6

Old	Change	New
2°C	−5°C	−3°C
	+7°C	2°C
	+6°C	−5°C
	−11°C	−1°C
	+15°C	10°C
	−10°C	−14°C

7

Old	Change	New
7°C		−3°C
−5°C		−19°C
−2°C		14°C
3°C		−6°C
0°C		−17°C
8°C		−1°C

On this page you will learn to extend number sequences.

> To find the rule that links the numbers, study the gaps.
>
> **Examples**
>
> 4   0   −4   −8   −12   The rule is 'subtract 4'.
> 1   4   7   10   13   The rule is 'add 3'.

A

Write the first six numbers in each sequence.

	Start at	Rule		Start at	Rule		Start at	Rule
1	23	+2	**6**	83	−7	**11**	21	+5
2	56	−8	**7**	59	+3	**12**	48	−6
3	125	+25	**8**	56	−7	**13**	19	+9
4	73	−5	**9**	5	+8	**14**	110	−20
5	47	+4	**10**	120	−3	**15**	21	+11

B

Complete these sequences by filling in the boxes. Write the rule each time.

1 83 85 87 89 ☐ ☐ ☐

2 −1 −3 −5 −7 ☐ ☐ ☐

3 ☐ ☐ ☐ 175 225 275 325

4 ☐ ☐ ☐ 61 72 83 94

5 68 64 ☐ ☐ ☐ 48 44

6 325 350 ☐ ☐ ☐ 450 475

7 0·2 0·4 0·6 0·8 ☐ ☐ ☐

8 −2 ☐ −10 ☐ −18 ☐ −26

9 ☐ 62 ☐ ☐ 47 42 37

10 2·1 1·8 ☐ 1·2 ☐ 0·6 ☐

11 62 ☐ 48 ☐ ☐ 27 20

12 ☐ 49 42 ☐ 28 21 ☐

13 114 ☐ 316 ☐ 518 ☐ 720

14 ☐ −40 ☐ ☐ −25 −20 −15

15 68 57 ☐ 35 ☐ 13 ☐

16 0·5 ☐ 1·5 ☐ ☐ 3·0 3·5

C

Copy these sequences and write the next three numbers. Write the rule each time.

1 77 83 89 95

2 −2 −4 −6 −8

3 0·1 0·3 0·5 0·7

4 68 77 86 95

5 25 20 15 10

6 35 60 85 110

7 3 1 −1 −3

8 0·25 0·5 0·75 1·0

9 132 121 110 99

10 0·05 0·06 0·07 0·08

11 54 62 70 78

12 18 14 10 6

13 4·8 3·8 2·8 1·8

14 45 38 31 24

15 64 52 40 28

16 5 24 43 62

17 19 13 7 1

18 48 69 90 111

On this page you will learn to recognise odd and even numbers and to give examples that match statements about odd or even numbers.

An even number is a number which can be divided exactly by 2.

An odd number cannot be divided by 2 without leaving a remainder.

Examples

16 ÷ 2 = 8   16 is an even number.

17 ÷ 2 = 8 remainder 1   17 is an odd number.

 A

| 123 | 136 | 487 | 318 | 524 | 631 |
| 269 | 312 | 885 | 918 | 263 | 574 |

1. Which of the above numbers is odd?
2. Which of the above numbers is even?
3. Give the next odd number after all of the above numbers.
4. Give the next even number after all of the above numbers.

Give three examples for each of the following questions.

5. If you add 2 even numbers, is the answer odd or even?
6. If you add 2 odd numbers, is the answer odd or even?
7. If you add an odd and an even number, is the answer odd or even? Is this always true?

B

The first five numbers in the 3 times table are:

| 3 | 6 | 9 | 12 | 15 |
| odd | even | odd | even | odd |

What is the pattern to the odds and evens in these tables?

1. 2s
2. 4s
3. 5s
4. 7s
5. 14s
6. 18s
7. 19s
8. 21s

C

Copy and complete these rules by writing odd or even in the box.

1. If you add three odd numbers the answer is always _____ .
2. If you add three even numbers the answer is always _____ .
3. If you add two odd and one even number the answers is always _____ .
4. If you add two even and one odd number the answers is always _____ .
5. Give four examples for each of the rules.

On this page you will learn to recognise multiples.

Multiples are the numbers in a multiplication table.

Example

The multiples of 2 are the numbers in the 2 times table.

2, 4, 6, 8, 10, 12, ... 34, 36, 38, 40, ... 122, 124, 126, 128 and so on.

A

Write down the first five multiples of:

1 4   **4** 6

2 5   **5** 9

3 10   **6** 20.

Write Yes or No.

7 Is 56 a multiple of 2?

8 Is 32 a multiple of 3?

9 Is 85 a multiple of 5?

10 Is 26 a multiple of 4?

11 Is 82 a multiple of 8?

12 Is 150 a multiple of 10?

13 Is 60 a multiple of 3?

14 Is 65 a multiple of 2?

15 Is 54 a multiple of 9?

16 Is 47 a multiple of 7?

17 Is 42 a multiple of 6?

18 Is 84 a multiple of 4?

19 Is 54 a multiple of 5?

20 Is 75 a multiple of 15?

21 Is 89 a multiple of 11?

22 Is 24 a multiple of 8?

23 Is 300 a multiple of 50?

24 Is 210 a multiple of 20?

B

Which number should not be in the box?

1 Multiples of 5
106, 80, 75, 135

2 Multiples of 8
48, 72, 54, 32

3 Multiples of 6
42, 36, 46, 54

4 Multiples of 9
81, 54, 69, 99

5 Multiples of 4
46, 16, 36, 56

6 Multiples of 7
70, 42, 56, 64

Find two numbers that are multiples of both:

7 2 and 7   **10** 4 and 5

8 3 and 4   **11** 3 and 10

9 3 and 5   **12** 4 and 6.

C

24   72   40   3

144   45   90

27   54   32   96

Write down the numbers on the cards which are multiples of:

1 3   **3** 8

2 6   **4** 9.

Find three numbers that are multiples of both:

5 2 and 9   **8** 4 and 7

6 3 and 8   **9** 5 and 6

7 8 and 10   **10** 6 and 8.

Use these digits.

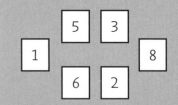

5   3

1   8

6   2

Make as many 2-digit numbers as you can that are multiples of:

11 2   **15** 7

12 3   **16** 9

13 5   **17** 4

14 8   **18** 6.

On this page you will learn to use tests of divisibility.

Whole numbers are divisible by:

> 100 if the last two digits are 00.
> 10 if the last digit is 0.
> 2 if the number is even.
> 4 if the last two digits are divisible by 4.
> 5 if the last digit is 0 or 5.
> 3 if the sum of the digits is divisible by 3.

A

Write True or False for each of the following statements.

1 300 is divisible by 100.   **6** 58 is divisible by 5.   **11** 814 is divisible by 4.

2 61 is divisible by 2.   **7** 32 is divisible by 2.   **12** 200 is divisible by 10.

3 320 is divisible by 5.   **8** 470 is divisible by 100.   **13** 50 is divisible by 100.

4 226 is divisible by 4.   **9** 340 is divisible by 4.   **14** 45 is divisible by 2.

5 40 is divisible by 10.   **10** 174 is divisible by 5.   **15** 136 is divisible by 4.

B

Write down which of these numbers is divisible by:

1 100	**2** 10	**3** 2	**4** 4	**5** 5
600	70	18	68	65
4040	65	94	422	312
320	900	247	784	830
1000	1320	1356	978	715
750	836	865	236	964

C

Copy and complete the table, using ticks and crosses to show divisibility.

Number	Divisible by				
	2	3	4	5	10
415	✗				
648	✓				
760					
834					
964					
1066					

On this page you will learn:

- **to identify factors.**

Factors are numbers that divide exactly into another number. It is often useful to think of factors as pairs of numbers whose product is the target number.

Examples

Find the factors of 12.   Find the factors of 9.

1×12 2×6 3×4 1×9 3×3

Factors of 12:   1, 2, 3, 4, 6, 12   Factors of 9:   1, 3, 9

- **to use factors for finding products.**

Examples $15 \times 6 = 3 \times 5 \times 6$ $23 \times 12 = 23 \times 3 \times 2 \times 2$
$$= 3 \times 30 \qquad\qquad = 69 \times 2 \times 2$$
$$= 90 \qquad\qquad\quad = 138 \times 2$$
$$= 276$$

A

Find different pairs of numbers whose product gives each of the following target numbers.
The number of different ways possible is shown in brackets.

1 6(2)   **3** 12(3)   **5** 15(2)   **7** 20(3)   **9** 16(3)   **11** 36(5)

2 8(2)   **4** 14(2)   **6** 18(3)   **8** 25(2)   **10** 40(4)   **12** 100(5)

B

Find all the factors of the following numbers.

1 16   **3** 30   **5** 48   **7** 80

2 21   **4** 54   **6** 77   **8** 64

Break the second number down into factors to help find these products.

9 24 × 6   **11** 16 × 12   **13** 24 × 9   **15** 22 × 18

10 15 × 8   **12** 21 × 14   **14** 18 × 15   **16** 32 × 16

C

The factors of 12:   1, 2, 3, 4, 6, 12   The highest factor shared
The factors of 16:   1, 2, 4, 8, 16   by both 12 and 16 is 4.

Find the highest factor shared by these pairs of numbers.

1 8 and 12   **3** 20 and 30   **5** 12 and 18   **7** 21 and 35   **9** 36 and 54

2 12 and 15   **4** 15 and 25   **6** 24 and 40   **8** 18 and 24   **10** 36 and 48

Break the second number down into factors to help find these products.

11 18 × 18   **12** 32 × 24   **13** 46 × 25   **14** 41 × 36   **15** 54 × 48

On this page you will learn to recognise square numbers.

When a number is multiplied by itself you get a square number.

Examples

Three squared $(3^2) = 3 \times 3 = 9$

$4^2 = 4 \times 4 = 16$

A

They are called square numbers because they make this pattern of squares.

$1^2 = 1 \times 1 = 1$

$2^2 = 2 \times 2 = 4$

$3^2 = 3 \times 3 = 9$

$4^2 = 4 \times 4 = 16$

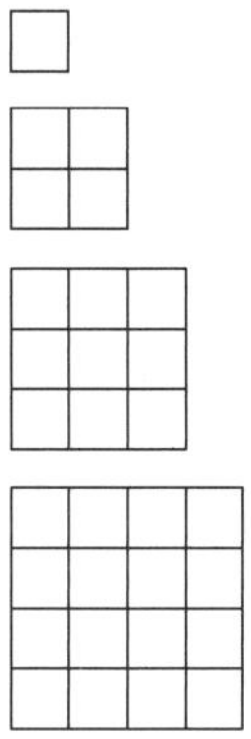

Using squared paper, continue the pattern above up to 10^2.

B

Continue this table up to 12^2.

$$1^2 = 1 \qquad\quad = 1$$
$$2^2 = 1 + 3 \qquad = 4$$
$$3^2 = 1 + 3 + 5 = 9$$

C

Work out

1. 5^2
2. 6^2
3. 7^2

4. 8^2
5. 11^2
6. 13^2

7. $4^2 + 3^2$
8. $5^2 + 6^2$
9. $9^2 - 7^2$

10. $10^2 - 8^2$
11. $8^2 - 6^2$
12. $7^2 + 9^2$

Use a calculator to find which number, when multiplied by itself, gives:

13. 400
14. 225
15. 196
16. 256

17. 324
18. 1600
19. 625
20. 900

21. 1444
22. 2209
23. 729
24. 2500

25. 7569
26. 17 956
27. 59 049
28. 174 724.

On this page you will learn to recognise equivalent fractions.

Equivalent fractions are fractions that look different but are the same.

Examples

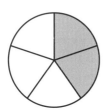

$$\frac{2}{5} = \frac{4}{10}$$

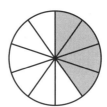

$$\frac{3}{4} = \frac{6}{8}$$

A

Write the equivalent fractions shown by the shaded areas in each pair of diagrams.

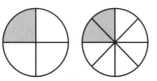

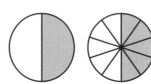

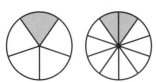

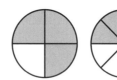

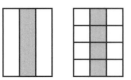

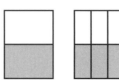

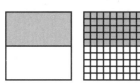

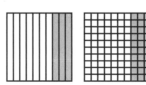

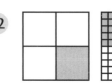

B

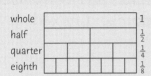

whole		1
half		$\frac{1}{2}$
quarter		$\frac{1}{4}$
eighth		$\frac{1}{8}$

whole		1
half		$\frac{1}{2}$
third		$\frac{1}{3}$
sixth		$\frac{1}{6}$

whole		1
half		$\frac{1}{2}$
fifth		$\frac{1}{5}$
tenth		$\frac{1}{10}$

Use the fraction charts. Copy and complete these equivalent fractions by filling in the box.

1   $\frac{1}{2} = \frac{\square}{8}$

4   $\frac{1}{4} = \frac{\square}{16}$

7   $\frac{5}{8} = \frac{\square}{16}$

10   $\frac{3}{4} = \frac{\square}{8}$

13   $\frac{1}{2} = \frac{\square}{16}$

2   $\frac{1}{3} = \frac{\square}{6}$

5   $\frac{1}{6} = \frac{\square}{12}$

8   $\frac{1}{2} = \frac{\square}{12}$

11   $\frac{2}{3} = \frac{\square}{12}$

14   $\frac{5}{6} = \frac{\square}{12}$

3   $\frac{3}{5} = \frac{\square}{10}$

6   $\frac{1}{10} = \frac{\square}{20}$

9   $\frac{7}{10} = \frac{\square}{20}$

12   $\frac{4}{5} = \frac{\square}{20}$

15   $\frac{3}{10} = \frac{\square}{20}$

Copy and complete these fraction chains.

16   $\frac{3}{4} = \frac{\square}{8} = \frac{\square}{12} = \frac{\square}{16} = \frac{\square}{\square} = \frac{\square}{\square}$

19   $\frac{1}{8} = \frac{2}{\square} = \frac{3}{\square} = \frac{\square}{\square} = \frac{\square}{\square} = \frac{\square}{\square}$

17   $\frac{1}{6} = \frac{2}{\square} = \frac{3}{\square} = \frac{4}{\square} = \frac{\square}{\square} = \frac{\square}{\square}$

20   $\frac{2}{3} = \frac{4}{6} = \frac{\square}{\square} = \frac{\square}{\square} = \frac{\square}{\square} = \frac{\square}{\square}$

18   $\frac{2}{5} = \frac{\square}{10} = \frac{\square}{15} = \frac{\square}{\square} = \frac{\square}{\square} = \frac{\square}{\square}$

21   $\frac{7}{10} = \frac{14}{20} = \frac{\square}{\square} = \frac{\square}{\square} = \frac{\square}{\square} = \frac{\square}{\square}$

C

You can change a fraction to an equivalent fraction:

BY CANCELLING

Example

$\frac{8}{12} \frac{(\div 4)}{(\div 4)} = \frac{2}{3}$

BY MULTIPLYING

Example

$\frac{2}{5} \frac{(\times 3)}{(\times 3)} = \frac{6}{15}$

Copy and complete these equivalent fractions by filling in the box.

1   $\frac{2}{3} = \frac{\square}{9}$

5   $\frac{4}{5} = \frac{\square}{25}$

9   $\frac{2}{5} = \frac{\square}{30}$

13   $\frac{\square}{10} = \frac{35}{50}$

17   $\frac{\square}{9} = \frac{8}{18}$

2   $\frac{1}{4} = \frac{\square}{20}$

6   $\frac{9}{10} = \frac{\square}{100}$

10   $\frac{1}{4} = \frac{\square}{60}$

14   $\frac{\square}{6} = \frac{15}{18}$

18   $\frac{\square}{3} = \frac{8}{12}$

3   $\frac{1}{2} = \frac{\square}{14}$

7   $\frac{1}{5} = \frac{\square}{100}$

11   $\frac{\square}{4} = \frac{9}{12}$

15   $\frac{\square}{5} = \frac{60}{100}$

19   $\frac{\square}{20} = \frac{40}{100}$

4   $\frac{1}{3} = \frac{\square}{18}$

8   $\frac{2}{3} = \frac{\square}{15}$

12   $\frac{\square}{5} = \frac{6}{15}$

16   $\frac{\square}{7} = \frac{20}{35}$

20   $\frac{\square}{8} = \frac{25}{40}$

Write three more fractions equivalent to:

21   $\frac{5}{13}$

22   $\frac{8}{36}$

23   $\frac{10}{24}$

24   $\frac{18}{33}$

25   $\frac{9}{16}$

26   $\frac{35}{40}$

27   $\frac{28}{60}$

28   $\frac{42}{150}$.

On this page you will learn to change an improper fraction to a mixed number and vice versa.

Examples

1. Change $\frac{7}{3}$ to a mixed number.

    Divide numerator by denominator. $7 \div 3 = 2$ rem. 1

    Put remainder over denominator. $\frac{7}{3} = 2\frac{1}{3}$

2. Change $4\frac{3}{8}$ to an improper fraction.

    Multiply whole number by denominator. $4 \times 8 = 32$

    Add the numerator. $32 + 3 = 35$

    Put sum over denominator. $4\frac{3}{8} = \frac{35}{8}$

A

Write the shaded areas as both mixed numbers and improper fractions.

1.
2.
3.
4.
5.
6.
7.
8.
9.
10.
11.
12.

B

Copy and complete.

1. $\frac{5}{3} = 1\frac{\square}{3}$

2. $\frac{7}{4} = \square\frac{3}{4}$

3. $\frac{19}{6} = \square\frac{\square}{6}$

4. $\frac{29}{10} = \square\frac{\square}{10}$

5. $\frac{25}{8} = \square\frac{\square}{\square}$

6. $\frac{421}{100} = \square\frac{\square}{\square}$

7. $3\frac{1}{2} = \frac{7}{\square}$

8. $2\frac{2}{3} = \frac{8}{\square}$

9. $5\frac{1}{4} = \frac{\square}{4}$

10. $4\frac{3}{5} = \frac{\square}{5}$

11. $3\frac{7}{10} = \frac{\square}{\square}$

12. $2\frac{5}{6} = \frac{\square}{\square}$

C

Change to mixed numbers.

1. $\frac{25}{4}$
2. $\frac{17}{3}$
3. $\frac{29}{6}$
4. $\frac{37}{7}$
5. $\frac{44}{5}$
6. $\frac{50}{8}$
7. $\frac{57}{9}$
8. $\frac{123}{10}$
9. $\frac{65}{12}$
10. $\frac{116}{50}$
11. $\frac{712}{100}$
12. $\frac{92}{25}$

Change to improper fractions.

13. $5\frac{1}{5}$
14. $5\frac{1}{3}$
15. $6\frac{3}{4}$
16. $9\frac{3}{6}$
17. $2\frac{6}{7}$
18. $7\frac{1}{8}$
19. $12\frac{9}{10}$
20. $3\frac{11}{12}$
21. $4\frac{7}{9}$
22. $7\frac{8}{100}$
23. $2\frac{11}{16}$
24. $9\frac{27}{50}$

On this page you will use your knowledge of equivalent fractions to compare and order fractions.

Example

Place $\frac{5}{12}, \frac{1}{3}, \frac{1}{2}$ in order, smallest first.

Convert the fractions to a common denominator. $\frac{1}{3} = \frac{4}{12}$ $\frac{1}{2} = \frac{6}{12}$

Arrange in order. $\frac{1}{3}, \frac{5}{12}, \frac{6}{12}$

A

$$\begin{array}{cccc} \dfrac{4}{10} & \dfrac{5}{8} & \dfrac{3}{6} & \dfrac{6}{10} \\[2ex] \dfrac{4}{8} & \dfrac{2}{6} & \dfrac{7}{12} & \dfrac{2}{5} \end{array}$$

Which of the fractions in the box are:

1. equal to one half?

2. less than one half?

3. greater than one half?

4. Match the fractions to the letters.

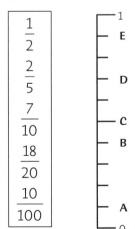

5. Write down the larger fraction.
   a) $\frac{1}{2}$ or $\frac{1}{3}$
   b) $\frac{3}{4}$ or $\frac{3}{8}$
   c) $\frac{1}{10}$ or $\frac{1}{5}$

B

Place in order, smallest first.

1. $\frac{3}{4}, \frac{1}{2}, \frac{3}{8}$

2. $\frac{1}{3}, \frac{1}{2}, \frac{1}{6}$

3. $\frac{3}{5}, \frac{1}{2}, \frac{7}{10}$

4. $\frac{11}{16}, \frac{3}{4}, \frac{5}{8}$

5. $\frac{2}{3}, \frac{5}{6}, \frac{9}{12}$

6. $\frac{2}{5}, \frac{5}{10}, \frac{9}{20}$

7. Match the fractions to the letters.

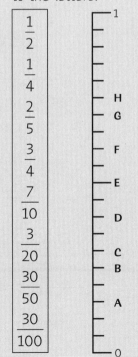

C

Find the fraction which is half way between each pair of numbers. You may find it helpful to use the fraction charts on page 18.

1. $\frac{1}{2}$ and 1

2. $\frac{1}{3}$ and $\frac{2}{3}$

3. $\frac{3}{5}$ and $\frac{4}{5}$

4. $\frac{1}{4}$ and $\frac{1}{2}$

5. $\frac{1}{3}$ and $\frac{1}{6}$

6. $\frac{3}{5}$ and $\frac{7}{10}$

7. $\frac{1}{2}$ and $\frac{3}{8}$

8. $\frac{2}{3}$ and $\frac{9}{12}$

9. $\frac{2}{5}$ and $\frac{9}{20}$

10. $\frac{1}{4}$ and $\frac{1}{3}$

11. Draw a 12 cm line with 24 marked divisions and mark on it these fractions.

$$\begin{array}{cccc} \dfrac{1}{2} & \dfrac{3}{8} & \dfrac{5}{6} & \dfrac{4}{12} \\[2ex] \dfrac{23}{24} & \dfrac{1}{12} & \dfrac{3}{4} & \dfrac{2}{3} \end{array}$$

On these pages you will learn what each digit in a decimal fraction represents.

Examples

three tenths
$\frac{3}{10} = 0.3$

fifty-seven hundredths
$\frac{57}{100} = 0.57$

The value of a digit depends upon its position in a number.

Each digit in a number is 10 times higher than the digit to the right. This applies to decimal fractions as well as to whole numbers.

	T	U	·	$\frac{1}{10}$	$\frac{1}{100}$	$\frac{1}{1000}$
30 =	3	0	·	0		
3 =		3	·	0		
$\frac{3}{10}$ =		0	·	3		
$\frac{3}{100}$ =		0	·	0	3	
$\frac{3}{1000}$ =		0	·	0	0	3

	T	U	·	$\frac{1}{10}$	$\frac{1}{100}$	$\frac{1}{1000}$
24 =	2	4	·	0		
$2\frac{4}{10}$ =		2	·	4		
$\frac{24}{100}$ =		0	·	2	4	
$\frac{24}{1000}$ =		0	·	0	2	4

A

What part of each shape is shaded?
Write your answer as a fraction and as a decimal fraction.

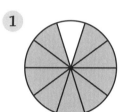

1   5

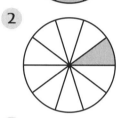

2   6

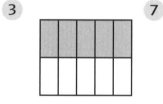

3   7

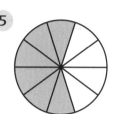

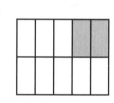

4   8

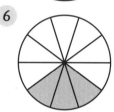

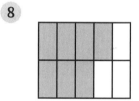

9 Write each number shown by the arrows as a decimal fraction.

Write each of these numbers as a decimal fraction.

10 $\frac{4}{10}$ **13** $2\frac{9}{10}$ **16** $10\frac{5}{10}$

11 $1\frac{7}{10}$ **14** $6\frac{8}{10}$ **17** $17\frac{2}{10}$

12 $3\frac{3}{10}$ **15** $\frac{6}{10}$ **18** $4\frac{1}{10}$

B

Express the shaded part of each diagram as a fraction and as a decimal fraction.

1   **3**

2   **4**

Write each number shown by the arrows as a decimal fraction.

5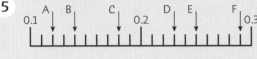

6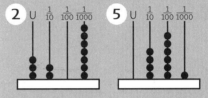

Give the value of the underlined figure in each of these numbers.

7 2·5<u>8</u>   **11** 13·3<u>2</u>   **15** 12·<u>4</u>1

8 <u>1</u>8·67   **12** 36·<u>9</u>   **16** 2·8<u>5</u>

9 <u>4</u>5·76   **13** 20·1<u>3</u>   **17** 1·6<u>1</u>

10 1<u>6</u>·53   **14** 7·9<u>2</u>   **18** 13·2<u>4</u>

Give the next five terms in each of these sequences.

19 0·01, 0·02, 0·03, 0·04, 0·05

20 1·0, 1·02, 1·04, 1·06, 1·08

21 1·92, 1·93, 1·94, 1·95, 1·96

22 0·91, 0·93, 0·95, 0·97, 0·99

23 0·6, 0·65, 0·7, 0·75, 0·8

24 4·07, 4·06, 4·05, 4·04, 4·03

C

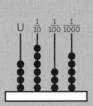

Example

$4 + \frac{6}{10} + \frac{3}{100} + \frac{5}{1000}$

4·635

Write the decimal fraction shown on each abacus.

1   **4**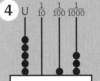

2   **5**

3   **6**

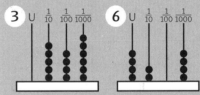

Write these numbers as decimal fractions.

7 $\frac{3}{100}$ **11** $\frac{72}{1000}$ **15** $1\frac{316}{1000}$

8 $\frac{263}{1000}$ **12** $\frac{451}{1000}$ **16** $6\frac{9}{100}$

9 $1\frac{18}{100}$ **13** $2\frac{96}{1000}$ **17** $1\frac{48}{1000}$

10 $5\frac{169}{1000}$ **14** $\frac{1}{1000}$ **18** $4\frac{5}{1000}$

Give the value of the underlined figure in each of these numbers.

19 4·<u>6</u>2   **23** 11·1<u>0</u>9   **27** 3·0<u>6</u>5

20 16·<u>7</u>91   **24** 33·3<u>3</u>   **28** 8·54<u>5</u>

21 18·13<u>5</u>   **25** 41·61<u>8</u>   **29** 0·0<u>1</u>6

22 <u>6</u>·472   **26** 1<u>9</u>·72   **30** 43·78<u>9</u>

On this page you will learn to order a set of decimals.

Write the set of decimals in a line with the decimal points in a column.
Fill in any empty spaces with zeros. This makes it easier to compare the decimals.

Example   Arrange 5·3, 0·35, 8 and 5·8 in order.

Write in column.	Put in zeros.	Arrange in order.
5·3	5·30	0·35
0·35	0·35	5·3
8	8·00	5·8
5·8	5·80	8

 A

Write the larger of these pairs of numbers.

1   1·7   7·0   **4**   21   2·1   **7**   7·0   3·7   **10**   5·4   4·5

2   35   5·3   **5**   1·0   1·1   **8**   0·3   3·0   **11**   7·5   57

3   4·0   2·4   **6**   2·5   25   **9**   8·0   6·8   **12**   1·5   5·0

13   Copy the number line. Put each number from the box on the line.

1·0   0·3   1·2   0·5   1·8   1·5

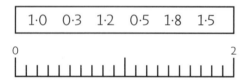

B

Arrange these decimals in order. Write the smallest first.

1   5·62, 6·52, 5·26, 6·5, 6·25   **5**   Copy the line and locate the numbers.

2   3·18, 1·8, 3·81, 3·8, 1·38

3   6·76, 6·6, 6·06, 6·7, 6·07

4   21·8, 2·8, 2·18, 2·08, 28

2·95   3·06   3·0   2·91   2·98   3·04

2·9   3·1

C

Arrange these decimals in order. Write the smallest first.

1   4·2, 4·25, 0·45, 4·5, 4·52   **5**   11·7, 1·71, 17·1, 1·17, 1·7

2   6·1, 6·71, 0·67, 6·7, 6·17   **6**   3·66, 3·36, 33·3, 3·63, 3·33

3   3·39, 0·93, 3·09, 0·39, 3·3   **7**   2·52, 2·2, 25·2, 22·5, 2·25

4   8·4, 8·22, 8·24, 8·44, 8·42   **8**   4·64, 4·646, 4·66, 4·464, 4·644

9   Draw a number line from 2·9 to 3·0 with 20 divisions. Put these numbers on your line.

2·95   2·99   2·91   2·975   2·925   2·94

On this page you will learn to round decimals to the nearest whole number.

To round a decimal fraction to the nearest whole number look at the tenths column.
If the number in that column is less than 5, round down.
If the number in that column is greater than 5, round up.

Examples

    3·5 rounds to 4   5·49 rounds to 5
    £2·70 rounds to £3   £6·28 rounds to £6

A

Copy and complete by choosing one of the numbers in the brackets.

1. 1·9 rounds to (1, 2).
2. 8·1 rounds to (8, 9).
3. 15·2 rounds to (15, 16).
4. 9·8 rounds to (9, 10).
5. 7·1 rounds to (7, 8).
6. 14·2 rounds to (14, 15).
7. 3·9 rounds to (3, 4).
8. 17·7 rounds to (17, 18).

Copy and complete by writing the correct amount in the box. Round to the nearest pound.

9. £12·30 rounds to ☐.
10. £5·80 rounds to ☐.
11. £6·10 rounds to ☐.
12. £3·90 rounds to ☐.
13. £7·20 rounds to ☐.
14. £8·60 rounds to ☐.
15. £4·50 rounds to ☐.
16. £3·40 rounds to ☐.

B

Round to the nearest whole number.

1. 4·8
2. 6·2
3. 3·5
4. 11·7
5. 8·4
6. 13·3
7. 0·52
8. 5·46

Round to the nearest pound.

9. £8·63
10. £27·27
11. £3·91
12. £6·36
13. £12·80
14. £7·52
15. £4·49
16. £9·78

Round to the nearest metre.

17. 5·6 m
18. 3·9 m
19. 9·7 m
20. 6·3 m
21. 2·8 m
22. 1·49 m
23. 7·5 m
24. 11·9 m

Round to the nearest kilogram.

25. 4·3 kg
26. 3·6 kg
27. 12·2 kg
28. 8·7 kg
29. 5·4 kg
30. 2·5 kg
31. 16·38 kg
32. 7·61 kg

C

1. Copy the table, rounding the miles to the nearest tenth.

Kilometres	Miles
1	0·62
2	1·24
3	1·86
4	2·49
5	3·11
6	3·73
7	4·35
8	4·97
9	5·59

2. Copy the table, rounding the gallons to the nearest 100 ml.

Litres	Gallons
1	0·22
2	0·44
3	0·66
4	0·88
5	1·10
6	1·32
7	1·54
8	1·76
9	1·98

FRACTIONS AND DECIMALS

On this page you will learn to recognise equivalent fractions and decimals.

It is important to remember that:

$$\frac{1}{10} = 0.1 \qquad \frac{2}{10} = 0.2 \qquad \frac{3}{10} = 0.3 \text{ and so on.}$$

$$\frac{1}{100} = 0.01 \qquad \frac{2}{100} = 0.02 \qquad \frac{3}{100} = 0.03 \text{ and so on.}$$

$$\frac{1}{2} = 0.5 \qquad \frac{1}{4} = 0.25 \qquad \frac{3}{4} = 0.75.$$

A

Write True or False for each of the following statements.

1. $\frac{9}{10} = 0.9$
2. $\frac{3}{4} = 0.34$
3. $\frac{1}{10} = 0.1$

4. $\frac{1}{2} = 0.2$
5. $\frac{3}{10} = 0.35$
6. $\frac{1}{4} = 0.4$

7. $\frac{7}{10} = 0.7$
8. $\frac{2}{10} = 2.0$
9. $0.25 = \frac{1}{4}$

10. $0.08 = \frac{8}{10}$
11. $0.75 = \frac{3}{4}$
12. $0.16 = \frac{6}{10}$

13. Match each of these fractions with one of these decimals.

$\frac{1}{2}$	0.14
$\frac{4}{10}$	0.2
$\frac{5}{100}$	0.25
$\frac{2}{10}$	0.5
$\frac{14}{100}$	0.4
$\frac{1}{4}$	0.05

B

Write as fractions.

1. 4.68
2. 1.17
3. 2.5
4. 4.3
5. 10.75
6. 6.59
7. 8.01
8. 8.1

Write as decimals.

9. £$1\frac{46}{100}$
10. £$2\frac{1}{4}$
11. £$5\frac{4}{100}$
12. £$3\frac{18}{100}$
13. $1\frac{4}{10}$ m
14. $3\frac{61}{100}$ m
15. $8\frac{3}{4}$ km
16. $17\frac{9}{100}$ km

Give the answer as a decimal.

17. $0.5 + \frac{4}{10}$
18. $\frac{31}{100} - 0.28$
19. $0.8 - \frac{1}{2}$
20. $\frac{3}{4} - 0.12$
21. $0.2 + \frac{1}{2}$
22. $\frac{1}{4} + 0.53$
23. $\frac{7}{10} - 0.3$
24. $\frac{94}{100} - 0.36$
25. $\frac{3}{10} + 0.47$

C

Write as fractions.

1. 1.34
2. 6.75
3. 8.4
4. 3.197
5. 2.06
6. 9.281
7. 0.714
8. 5.082
9. 3.007
10. 12.51
11. 16.932
12. 1.046

Write as decimals.

13. $1\frac{9}{100}$
14. $8\frac{1}{4}$
15. $2\frac{1}{5}$
16. $3\frac{517}{1000}$
17. £$\frac{7}{100}$
18. £$1\frac{3}{20}$
19. £$4\frac{3}{5}$
20. £$6\frac{7}{50}$
21. $2\frac{9}{100}$ m
22. $\frac{76}{1000}$ km
23. $1\frac{8}{1000}$ km
24. $\frac{7}{20}$ m

Write in ascending order.

25. $\frac{3}{4}$ 0.43 0.344
26. 0.91 $\frac{19}{100}$ $\frac{9}{10}$
27. $\frac{3}{5}$ 0.5 $\frac{27}{100}$
28. $\frac{81}{100}$ 0.188 0.8
29. $\frac{2}{7}$ 0.2 $\frac{27}{100}$
30. 0.56 $\frac{5}{6}$ 0.556
31. 0.311 $\frac{3}{10}$ $\frac{1}{3}$
32. $\frac{11}{100}$ 0.1 $\frac{101}{1000}$

On this page you will learn to find a fraction of a number or quantity.

Examples

$\frac{1}{8}$ of 640 = 640 ÷ 8
= 80

$\frac{3}{10}$ of 90 = (90 ÷ 10) × 3
= 9 × 3 = 27

To find what fraction one quantity is of another, make a fraction by putting one quantity over the other.

TAKE CARE! The units of the two quantities must be the same.

Example

What fraction of £2 is 50p?

Answer = $\frac{50}{200} = \frac{1}{4}$, because £2 = 200p.

A

Find $\frac{1}{10}$ of:

1. 30
2. 80
3. 20
4. 50
5. 70 cm
6. 1 m
7. 40p
8. £1·00.

Find $\frac{1}{5}$ of:

9. 10
10. 30
11. 25
12. 45
13. 15 cm
14. 50 cm
15. 40p
16. 35p.

Find $\frac{1}{3}$ of:

17. 9
18. 15
19. 21
20. 12
21. 18 cm
22. 27 cm
23. 30p
24. 24p.

Find $\frac{1}{4}$ of:

25. 8
26. 32
27. 24
28. 36
29. 16 cm
30. 28 cm
31. 40p
32. 20p.

B

Find

1. $\frac{1}{10}$ of 400
2. $\frac{3}{10}$ of 70
3. $\frac{3}{5}$ of 45
4. $\frac{9}{10}$ of 60
5. $\frac{1}{10}$ of 350
6. $\frac{1}{6}$ of 42
7. $\frac{1}{5}$ of 1 m
8. $\frac{3}{4}$ of 48 cm
9. $\frac{7}{10}$ of 1 m
10. $\frac{2}{3}$ of 75p
11. $\frac{1}{4}$ of £1
12. $\frac{43}{100}$ of £1

What fraction of £1 is:

13. 10p
14. 5p
15. 35p
16. 80p?

What fraction of 1 km is:

17. 50 m
18. 200 m
19. 250 m
20. 750 m?

What fraction of 1 day is:

21. 1 hour
22. 4 hours
23. 6 hours
24. 8 hours?

C

Find

1. $\frac{7}{10}$ of 400
2. $\frac{4}{5}$ of 60
3. $\frac{5}{6}$ of 120
4. $\frac{3}{10}$ of 6 m
5. $\frac{73}{100}$ of 3 m
6. $\frac{81}{1000}$ of 1 m
7. $\frac{311}{1000}$ of 1 kg
8. $\frac{9}{10}$ of 4 kg
9. $\frac{7}{100}$ of 2 kg
10. $\frac{3}{5}$ of 1 litre
11. $\frac{7}{8}$ of 400 ml
12. $\frac{4}{7}$ of 56 litres

What fraction of £1 is:

13. 2p
14. 45p
15. 99p
16. £1·20?

What fraction of 1 km is:

17. 20 m
18. 125 m
19. 800 m
20. 500 m?

What fraction of 1 year is:

21. 1 day
22. 1 week
23. 5 weeks
24. June?

On these pages you will learn:

- **to understand percentage as the number of parts in 100.**

Per cent means out of 100.
Percentages are fractions with a
denominator of 100.
The symbol for per cent is %.

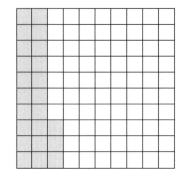

23 small squares are shaded.

Fraction shaded $= \frac{23}{100}$.

Percentage shaded = 23%.

- **to recognise when percentages, decimals and fractions are equal.**

To express fractions as percentages, change them to equivalent fractions with denominators of 100.

Example

$\frac{3}{10} = \frac{30}{100} = 30\%$

To express decimals as percentages, multiply by 100.

Example

$0{\cdot}53 = 53\%$

You need to know that:

$1 = \frac{100}{100} = 1{\cdot}0 = 100\%$

$\frac{1}{10} = \frac{10}{100} = 0{\cdot}1 = 10\%$

$\frac{1}{5} = \frac{20}{100} = 0{\cdot}2 = 20\%$

$\frac{1}{100} = \frac{1}{100} = 0{\cdot}01 = 1\%$

$\frac{1}{4} = \frac{25}{100} = 0{\cdot}25 = 25\%$

$\frac{1}{2} = \frac{50}{100} = 0{\cdot}5 = 50\%$

$\frac{3}{4} = \frac{75}{100} = 0{\cdot}75 = 75\%$

A

Use 10 × 10 grids of small squares. Shade in:

1 27 squares **3** 9 squares

2 80 squares **4** 50 squares.

Express each shaded area as:
a) a fraction
b) a decimal
c) a percentage.

5 Copy and complete the table.

Fraction	Decimal	Percentage
$\frac{1}{2}$		
$\frac{1}{10}$		
1		
$\frac{1}{4}$		
$\frac{3}{4}$		
$\frac{1}{100}$		

Copy the sentences changing each fraction to a percentage.

6 *One tenth* of the cars were blue.

7 Ellie has read *three quarters* of her book.

8 *One half* of the class saw the programme.

9 *One pence* is *one hundredth* of one pound.

10 Bruce lost *one fifth* of his golf balls.

B

Express each shaded area as:
a) a fraction
b) a decimal
c) a percentage.

1

4

7

10

2

5

8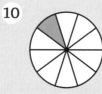

11

3

6

9

12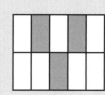

C

Write each fraction as:
a) a decimal
b) a percentage.

Write each percentage as:
a) a fraction in its simplest form
b) a decimal.

1 $\frac{1}{10}$ **3** $\frac{1}{100}$ **5** $\frac{7}{100}$ **7** $\frac{2}{5}$ **9** 50% **11** 9% **13** 80% **15** 75%

2 $\frac{3}{10}$ **4** $\frac{69}{100}$ **6** $\frac{1}{5}$ **8** $\frac{1}{4}$ **10** 91% **12** 90% **14** 95% **16** 39%

17 83% of the passengers on a coach are children. What percentage are adults?

18 41% of the footballers in the Premiership are foreign.
What percentage are English?

19 Copy the table but give each of the marks achieved as a percentage of the total marks for that test.

Subject	Total	Alison	Gary	Carly	Lee
English	100	61	39	58	47
Maths	200	140	168	70	94
Science	50	23	36	39	42
Geography	20	12	11	15	14
History	25	20	19	16	13

On this page you will learn:

● to find percentages of numbers.　　● to find percentages by halving.

Examples

25% of $36 = \frac{1}{4}$ of 36
$$= 9$$

30% of £1 $= \frac{3}{10}$ of £1
$$= 30p$$

Examples

Find 75% of £500.

100% of £500 $=$ £500
50% of £500 $=$ £250
25% of £500 $=$ £125
75% of £500 $=$ £375

A

Find 10% of:

1　30
4　40
2　90
5　100
3　60
6　70.

Find 50% of:

7　18
10　200
8　50
11　48
9　42
12　70.

Find 25% of:

13　16
16　100
14　40
17　32
15　24
18　200.

Find 20% of:

19　20
22　50
20　30
23　60
21　100
24　150.

Work out 25% of the following amounts of money by halving.

25　£12·00
28　£8·80
26　36p
29　64p
27　80p
30　£1·60

B

Work out

1　10% of 60
2　50% of 36
3　25% of 48
4　20% of 45
5　30% of 120
6　10% of 200
7　75% of 40
8　40% of 80
9　50% of £3·00
10　20% of 15p
11　10% of £1·40
12　25% of £1·20
13　30% of £2·20
14　75% of £5·00
15　40% of £1·50
16　40% of £3·30

Work out 75% of the following amounts of money by halving.

17　£200
20　48p
18　60p
21　£36·00
19　£2·80
22　84p

C

Copy and complete.

1　10% of ☐ = 4
2　20% of ☐ = 28
3　25% of ☐ = 20
4　40% of ☐ = 8
5　70% of ☐ = 28
6　50% of ☐ = 37
7　60% of ☐ = 30
8　1% of ☐ = 0·5
9　20% of ☐ = 50
10　75% of ☐ = 60
11　5% of ☐ = 10
12　80% of ☐ = 16
13　30% of ☐ = 24
14　10% of ☐ = 2·5
15　1% of ☐ = 1·3
16　2% of ☐ = 4

Work out 12·5% of the following amounts of money by halving.

17　£500
20　£1·20
18　80p
21　72p
19　£112
22　£6·40

On this page you will solve simple problems involving ratio and proportion.

A

A television programme is shown on three days in every week. Copy and complete the table.

1

Number of weeks	1	2	3	4	5	6	7	8	9	10
Number of programmes	3									

2 Make a similar table for a programme which is shown every day of the week.

B

Copy and complete these sentences for each of the patterns below.

a) For every one shaded square there is/are ☐ white square(s).
b) 1 in every ☐ squares is shaded.

1
3
5

2
4
6

C

1 Michael has four stamps for every three Sandra has.
Michael has 600 stamps. How many stamps does Sandra have?

2 In a class of 30 there are two fair-haired children to every
three with darker hair. How many children have fair hair?

3 There are 60 apples in a box. Two in every five apples are red.
The rest are green. How many green apples are there?

4 Bradley has six times as many conkers as Sandeep.
Sandeep has 8 conkers. How many does Bradley have?

5 During the season the school football team scored five goals to every four scored by their
opponents. 63 goals were scored in the matches. How many goals were scored by the
school team?

6 There were 40 passengers on a bus. Three in every eight sat upstairs.
How many passengers sat downstairs?

7 A shop sells 8 times as many white shirts as black shirts.
72 white shirts are sold. How many black shirts are sold?

8 A farmer has 5 sheep for every 2 cows.
He has 300 sheep. How many cows does he have?

On this page you will learn to understand the vocabulary and operation of addition.

---

153 + 118 can be expressed in different ways.

the sum of 153 and 118	153 add 118
the total of 153 and 118	153 plus 118
153 and 118 added together	118 greater than 153
153 increased by 118	118 more than 153.

A

Work out

1. 37 add 26.
2. The sum of 800 and 600.
3. 52 plus 30.
4. 230 increased by 64.
5. The total of 28 and 45.
6. 19 greater than 35.

7. 78 and 43 added together.
8. 31 more than 67.
9. 400 added to 553.
10. 4196 increased by 7.
11. The sum of 46 and 46.
12. 57 plus 26.

B

Copy and complete by writing the missing number in the box.

1. 47 added to ☐ is 100.
2. ☐ plus 61 is 134.
3. 0·4 increased by ☐ is 1.
4. The sum of ☐ and 360 is 630.
5. 600 greater than ☐ is 1395.
6. 2·3 and ☐ added together is 5·8.

7. The total of ☐ and 39 is 114.
8. 130 more than ☐ is 775.
9. 250 add ☐ is 1000.
10. 6·5 plus ☐ is 10.
11. 5·8 increased by ☐ is 6.
12. The total of 747 and ☐ is 800.

C

Copy and complete by writing the missing number in the box.

1. $4·68 + \square = 5$
2. $2700 + \square = 5600$
3. $0·72 + \square = 0·92$
4. $4400 + \square = 8100$

5. $4·37 + \square = 4·4$
6. $1·3 + \square = 2·67$
7. $\square + 3600 = 8400$
8. $\square + 0·31 = 7$

9. $\square + 2·9 = 57$
10. $\square + 0·06 = 0·26$
11. $\square + 2·1 = 8·3$
12. $\square + 0·5 = 0·89$

13. Find all the different totals you can make using three of these five numbers.

2917   163   7   4307   83

On this page you will learn to understand the vocabulary and operation of subtraction.

TAKING AWAY.
9 take away 4.
9 subtract 4.
9 decreased by 4.

FINDING A DIFFERENCE.
The difference between 9 and 4.
How many more is 9 than 4?
How many less is 4 than 9?

THE INVERSE OF ADDITION.
Find the missing number. $\square - 360 = 270$
The answer is 630 because $270 + 360 = 630$.

A

Work out

1 Take 550 from 1000.
2 57 less than 63.
3 94 subtract 39.
4 144 decreased by 53.
5 8000 take away 7991.
6 7 less than 5000.
7 Subtract 21 from 157.
8 120 take away 50.
9 Decrease 401 by 395.
10 Take 34 from 100.
11 700 less than 1500.
12 77 subtract 34.

B

Copy and complete by writing the missing number in the box.

1 $\square$ take away 8·3 is 0·7.
2 1·0 take away $\square$ is 0·6.
3 $\square$ subtract 61 is 774.
4 583 subtract $\square$ is 343.
5 $\square$ is 49 more than 533.
6 0·52 is $\square$ more than 0·15.
7 $\square$ decreased by 187 is 115.
8 10 decreased by $\square$ is 6·3.
9 $\square$ take away 2996 is 2007.
10 820 take away $\square$ is 250.
11 $\square$ is 600 less than 1325.
12 7·2 is $\square$ less than 9·1.

C

Find the difference between these numbers and:

10	2·9	2·1
1 3·2	5 5·1	9 4·0
2 7·5	6 8·3	10 6·6
3 6·9	7 11·7	11 9·2
4 5·4	8 7·4	12 13·8

Copy and complete by writing the missing number in the box.

13 $\square - 2600 = 5600$
14 $5000 - \square = 1765$
15 $\square - 1·9 = 6·6$
16 $7·0 - \square = 4·28$
17 $\square - 3700 = 3800$
18 $10·0 - \square = 4·3$
19 $\square - 3·1 = 1·4$
20 $8000 - \square = 2907$
21 $\square - 0·9 = 7·2$
22 $0·83 - \square = 0·73$

On this page you will practise using addition facts.

A

Work out

1. $70 + 80$
2. $90 + 60$
3. $90 + 90$
4. $70 + 70$
5. $50 + 90$
6. $80 + 90$
7. $800 + 800$
8. $900 + 700$
9. $800 + 700$
10. $600 + 800$
11. $900 + 800$
12. $700 + 600$

13. Take one number from each box. Find all six calculations.
    Example
    $82 + 18 = 100$
    a)

82		66
53		82
26	+	18	= 100
18		47
65		74
34		35

b)

750		950
50		250
950	+	550	= 1000
250		450
450		50
550		750

B

Work out

1. $600 + 900$
2. $700 + 700$
3. $900 + 700$
4. $800 + 600$
5. $700 + 800$
6. $500 + 900$
7. $0.9 + 0.9$
8. $0.6 + 0.7$
9. $0.7 + 0.9$
10. $0.8 + 0.8$
11. $0.9 + 0.8$
12. $0.8 + 0.7$

13. Take one number from each box. Find all six calculations.
    Example
    $0.5 + 0.5 = 1.0$
    a)

0.5		0.4
0.1		0.8
0.6		0.2
0.2	+	0.6	= 1.0
0.8		0.9
0.4		0.5

b)

2.7		6.2
8.3		7.3
1.5		3.6
5.9	+	1.7	= 10.0
6.4		8.5
3.8		4.1

C

Copy and complete.

1. $41 + \square = 100$
2. $37 + \square = 100$
3. $84 + \square = 100$
4. $16 + \square = 100$

5. $260 + \square = 1000$
6. $650 + \square = 1000$
7. $590 + \square = 1000$
8. $70 + \square = 1000$

9. $7200 + \square = 10\,000$
10. $1300 + \square = 10\,000$
11. $800 + \square = 10\,000$
12. $5600 + \square = 10\,000$

13. What needs to be added to each number in the outer ring to make the target number?
    Example
    $0.27 + 0.73 = 1.0$
    a)

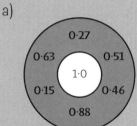

b)

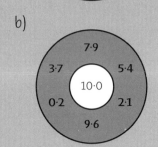

On this page you will practise using subtraction facts.

A

Work out

1. $150 - \square = 80$
2. $160 - \square = 70$
3. $170 - \square = 90$
4. $150 - \square = 60$
5. $140 - \square = 80$
6. $160 - \square = 90$
7. $1800 - \square = 900$
8. $1300 - \square = 800$
9. $1500 - \square = 900$
10. $1700 - \square = 800$
11. $1600 - \square = 800$
12. $1400 - \square = 500$

13. Take one number from each box. Find all six calculations.
Example
$100 - 49 = 51$

a)

$$100- \begin{array}{|c|} \hline 49 \\ 51 \\ 13 \\ 26 \\ 74 \\ 67 \\ \hline \end{array} = \begin{array}{|c|} \hline 33 \\ 49 \\ 74 \\ 26 \\ 51 \\ 87 \\ \hline \end{array}$$

b)

$$1000- \begin{array}{|c|} \hline 350 \\ 550 \\ 650 \\ 850 \\ 150 \\ 250 \\ \hline \end{array} = \begin{array}{|c|} \hline 450 \\ 750 \\ 850 \\ 350 \\ 150 \\ 650 \\ \hline \end{array}$$

B

Work out

1. $1500 - \square = 600$
2. $1700 - \square = 900$
3. $1600 - \square = 900$
4. $1500 - \square = 700$
5. $1.6 - \square = 0.7$
6. $1.4 - \square = 0.9$
7. $1.7 - \square = 0.8$
8. $1.5 - \square = 0.8$
9. $1.8 - \square = 0.9$
10. $1.6 - \square = 0.8$
11. $1.3 - \square = 0.6$
12. $1.5 - \square = 0.9$

13. Take one number from each box. Find all six calculations.
Example
$1.0 - 0.2 = 0.8$

a)

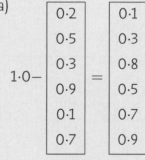

$$1.0- \begin{array}{|c|} \hline 0.2 \\ 0.5 \\ 0.3 \\ 0.9 \\ 0.1 \\ 0.7 \\ \hline \end{array} = \begin{array}{|c|} \hline 0.1 \\ 0.3 \\ 0.8 \\ 0.5 \\ 0.7 \\ 0.9 \\ \hline \end{array}$$

b)

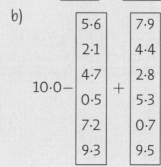

$$10.0- \begin{array}{|c|} \hline 5.6 \\ 2.1 \\ 4.7 \\ 0.5 \\ 7.2 \\ 9.3 \\ \hline \end{array} + \begin{array}{|c|} \hline 7.9 \\ 4.4 \\ 2.8 \\ 5.3 \\ 0.7 \\ 9.5 \\ \hline \end{array}$$

C

Copy and complete.

1. $100 - \square = 72$
2. $100 - \square = 35$
3. $100 - \square = 51$
4. $100 - \square = 29$
5. $1000 - \square = 630$
6. $1000 - \square = 480$
7. $1000 - \square = 140$
8. $1000 - \square = 960$
9. $10\,000 - \square = 8300$
10. $10\,000 - \square = 700$
11. $10\,000 - \square = 4800$
12. $10\,000 - \square = 1500$

13. Find the difference between each number in the outer ring and the target number.
Example
$1.0 - 0.81 = 0.19$

a)

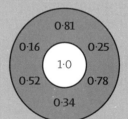

b)

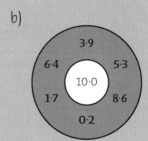

On this page you will learn to find a difference by counting up through the next multiple of 10, 100 or 1000.

Examples

$$403 - 186 = 4 + 10 + 200 + 3$$
$$= 217$$

$$7003 - 3995 = 5 + 3000 + 3$$
$$= 3008$$

A

Work out

1 $74 - 67$

2 $63 - 54$

3 $402 - 285$

4 $6000 - 5986$

5 $72 - 38$

6 $303 - 177$

7 $506 - 287$

8 $705 - 369$

9 $5000 - 4974$

10 $7000 - 6965$

B

Work out

1 $503 - 194$

2 $702 - 279$

3 $8004 - 5991$

4 $6000 - 2982$

5 $614 - 396$

6 $815 - 479$

7 $9000 - 3846$

8 $7005 - 1987$

9 $6013 - 3988$

10 $8000 - 4777$

C

Copy and complete.

1 $728 - \square = 291$

2 $532 - \square = 176$

3 $641 - \square = 383$

4 $8000 - \square = 2785$

5 $5000 - \square = 1784$

6 $7000 - \square = 3869$

7 $6004 - \square = 3965$

8 $836 - \square = 268$

9 $8000 - \square = 5677$

10 $7005 - \square = 3974$

Now you will learn to partition into 100s, 10s and 1s.

Examples

$$279 - 45 = 279 - 40 - 5$$
$$= 239 - 5$$
$$= 234$$

$$328 + 63 = 320 + 60 + 8 + 3$$
$$= 380 + 11$$
$$= 391$$

A

Work out

1 $24 + 47$

2 $39 + 55$

3 $69 - 36$

4 $87 - 33$

5 $48 + 39$

6 $57 + 26$

7 $78 - 43$

8 $96 - 22$

9 $74 - 36$

10 $83 - 58$

B

Work out

1 $239 + 54$

2 $516 + 47$

3 $347 - 54$

4 $539 - 65$

5 $348 + 39$

6 $627 + 68$

7 $426 - 44$

8 $618 - 67$

9 $263 - 58$

10 $454 - 27$

C

Copy and complete.

1 $376 - \square = 57$

2 $428 - \square = 143$

3 $\square + 189 = 446$

4 $269 - \square = 86$

5 $546 - \square = 152$

6 $\square + 652 = 866$

7 $157 - \square = 67$

8 $369 - \square = 193$

9 $\square + 168 = 533$

10 $484 - \square = 79$

On this page you will learn to identify near doubles.

Example

$$2.5 + 2.6 = (2.5 \times 2) + 0.1$$
$$= 5.0 + 0.1$$
$$= 5.1$$

A

Work out

1. $1.2 + 1.3$
2. $2.1 + 2.2$
3. $2.3 + 2.4$
4. $1.4 + 1.3$
5. $3.4 + 3.5$
6. $1.1 + 1.3$
7. $3.3 + 3.2$
8. $4.2 + 4.4$
9. $2.3 + 2.1$
10. $3.3 + 3.4$

B

Work out

1. $1.5 + 1.6$
2. $2.5 + 2.7$
3. $3.5 + 3.4$
4. $4.5 + 4.6$
5. $1.5 + 1.4$
6. $2.5 + 2.4$
7. $3.5 + 3.7$
8. $4.5 + 4.3$
9. $2.5 + 2.8$
10. $3.5 + 3.6$

C

Copy and complete.

1. $2.8 + \square = 5.6$
2. $3.7 + \square = 7.6$
3. $4.8 + \square = 9.4$
4. $5.7 + \square = 11.5$
5. $3.8 + \square = 7.4$
6. $2.6 + \square = 5.3$
7. $4.6 + \square = 9.3$
8. $5.9 + \square = 11.7$
9. $7.7 + \square = 15.2$
10. $6.8 + \square = 13.7$

Now you will learn to add or subtract using the nearest multiple of 10, 100 or 1000.

Examples

$$357 + 61 = 357 + 60 + 1$$
$$= 417 + 1$$
$$= 418$$

$$264 + 98 = 264 + 100 - 2$$
$$= 364 - 2$$
$$= 362$$

$$5008 - 1994 = 5008 - 2000 + 6$$
$$= 3008 + 6$$
$$= 3014$$

A

Work out

1. $63 + 29$ ✓
2. $75 - 19$
3. $93 + 61$ ✓
4. $193 - 71$
5. $84 + 28$ ✓
6. $129 - 63$
7. $88 + 71$ ✓
8. $97 - 29$
9. $96 + 43$ ✓
10. $137 - 48$

B

Work out

1. $468 + 81$
2. $467 - 71$
3. $284 + 99$
4. $379 - 98$
5. $453 + 102$
6. $625 - 49$
7. $5002 + 2998$
8. $4007 - 3006$
9. $6005 + 2007$
10. $3004 - 1997$

C

Copy and complete.

1. $\square + 199 = 648$
2. $\square - 299 = 364$
3. $\square + 2986 = 8279$
4. $\square + 111 = 983$
5. $\square - 202 = 627$
6. $\square + 3012 = 5828$
7. $\square + 113 = 836$
8. $\square - 198 = 573$
9. $\square + 2015 = 6364$
10. $\square + 298 = 765$

On this page you will learn to use the relationship between addition and subtraction.

If you know one addition or subtraction
fact you can state three other related facts.

Example

$347 − 164 = 183$ $347 − 183 = 164$

$183 + 164 = 347$ $164 + 183 = 347$

A

Copy and complete.
Use the 3 given numbers only.

1 $34 + 27 = 61$

$\square + \square = \square$

$61 − \square = \square$

$\square − \square = 27$

2 $84 − \square = 26$

$84 − \square = \square$

$\square + \square = \square$

$\square + 58 = \square$

3 $\square + 48 = \square$

$\square + \square = 67$

$\square − \square = \square$

$\square − \square = 19$

4 $\square − \square = 36$

$91 − \square = \square$

$\square + 55 = \square$

$\square + \square = \square$

B

Work out and write
three related facts.

1 $124 + 217$

2 $106 − 43$

3 $168 + 39$

4 $293 − 52$

5 $340 + 160$

6 $800 − 370$

7 $14·6 + 7·9$

8 $3·9 − 1·4$

C

For each set of numbers
write four + or − facts.

1 $136, 118, 254$

2 $206, 149, 57$

3 $380, 1020, 640$

4 $1·8, 6·4, 4·6$

5 $417, 646, 229$

6 $303, 235, 68$

7 $260, 470, 730$

8 $2·3, 1·2, 3·5$

Now you will learn to use a variety of strategies to add several numbers.

Look for pairs that make 10 or 100.

Start with the largest number.

Recognise an equivalent multiplication.

Example $60 + 30 + 20 + 70 + 80$

Example $5 + 7 + 28 + 4$

Example $21 + 22 + 22 + 23 = 22 × 4$

Check your totals by adding in reverse order.

A

Add up each set of
numbers.

1 $4, 7, 9, 3$

2 $4, 3, 5, 4$

3 $8, 4, 17$

4 $80, 90, 10$

5 $5, 6, 7, 6$

6 $3, 8, 7, 2, 4$

7 $3, 2, 3, 4$

8 $9, 7, 12$

9 $20, 70, 80$

10 $1, 8, 5, 9, 5$

B

Add up each set of
numbers.

1 $17, 26, 13$

2 $30, 28, 30, 32$

3 $3, 4, 8, 5, 7$

4 $5, 8, 13, 3$

5 $23, 25, 27, 29$

6 $2, 4, 7, 6, 9$

7 $3, 18, 14, 16$

8 $40, 70, 90$

9 $16, 18, 20, 22, 24$

10 $30, 50, 60, 70$

C

Copy and complete by writing
the missing number in the box.

1 $\square + 8 + 16 + 9 = 40$

2 $12 + 19 + 18 + \square = 61$

3 $60 + 40 + \square + 70 = 240$

4 $8 + 6 + 9 + 2 + \square = 32$

5 $39 + \square + 40 + 41 = 135$

6 $90 + \square + 60 + 40 = 280$

7 $80 + \square + 50 + 20 = 200$

8 $22 + 23 + \square + 22 = 89$

9 $5 + \square + 19 + 28 + 7 = 68$

10 $24 + \square + 13 + 46 = 94$

On this page you will use strategies to add or subtract pairs of numbers.

A

Copy and complete the squares.

1

+	30	40	50
70		110	
42			
90			

2

−	60	90	70
120	60		
97			27
150			

3

+	60	250	430
37			
18	78		
24			

4

−	7	9	6
261			255
803			
374			

5

+	26	42	39
33			
48			
27			69

6

−	26	18	45
87			42
51			
93			

B

Write the answers only.

1. $460 + 370$
2. $630 - 290$
3. $1352 - 600$
4. $3·9 + 2·3$
5. $3002 - 2987$
6. $856 - 430$
7. $6005 - 5897$
8. $856 + 400$
9. $0·75 - 0·38$
10. $580 - 270$
11. $750 - 480$
12. $5002 - 4984$
13. $682 - 340$
14. $3·6 + 4·8$
15. $240 + 328$
16. $6·5 - 2·9$

Add 61.   Add 270.

17. 325   20. 560
18. 172   21. 218
19. 696   22. 390

Take 49.   Take 420.

23. 467   26. 642
24. 204   27. 910
25. 831   28. 785

Make 1.   Make 1000.

29. 0·2   32. 570
30. 0·45   33. 710
31. 0·75   34. 150

C

Copy and complete.

1. $\square + 4600 = 8300$
2. $\square - 3200 = 5900$
3. $0·3 + \square = 0·75$
4. $\square - 0·41 = 0·39$
5. $\square + 5300 = 9700$
6. $8400 - \square = 5800$
7. $4·74 + \square = 5$
8. $4·51 + \square = 4·6$
9. $0·16 + \square = 0·66$
10. $6200 - \square = 3800$
11. $0·7 - \square = 0·37$
12. $\square + 0·07 = 8·3$
13. $\square - 1700 = 7600$
14. $\square + 2500 = 6200$
15. $4800 + \square = 8200$
16. $\square + 0·38 = 9$
17. $\square - 0·55 = 0·28$
18. $\square + 3700 = 8300$

Copy and complete the squares.

19

+	0·6	0·16	1·66
0·3			
0·13		0·29	
0·05			

20

−	0·3	0·9	0·05
2·0		1·1	
4·6			
8·45			

On this page you will learn two informal methods for addition.

ADD LARGEST VALUE DIGITS FIRST

Example

```
   735        2384
+  458      +  729
   1100        2000
     80        1000
     13         100
   1193          13
              3113
```

COMPENSATION

Example

```
   865
+  278
   1165    (865 + 300)
-    22    (278 − 300)
   1143
```

A

Use both methods for each sum.

1. 346
    + 38

5. 437
    + 92

2. 472
    + 57

6. 563
    + 89

3. 258
    + 45

7. 417
    + 65

4. 690
    + 76

8. 735
    + 77

9. Adam needs 219 first class stamps and 56 second class stamps. How many stamps does he need altogether?

B

Use both methods for each sum.

1. 674
    + 148

5. 784
    + 293

2. 493
    + 239

6. 567
    + 186

3. 848
    + 671

7. 925
    + 578

4. 2086
    + 275

8. 1289
    + 345

9. There are 384 boys and 356 girls in a Secondary School. How many pupils are there altogether?

10. Ebony was returning home to the United States of America. She flew 3168 miles and then drove 179 miles. How long was her journey?

C

Add largest value digits first. Set out as in the examples.

1. 3485 + 789
2. 6879 + 2967
3. 7094 + 2845
4. 5876 + 975
5. 3468 + 1376
6. 5925 + 438

Use compensation. Set out as in the example.

7. 6705 + 1836
8. 6751 + 654
9. 8368 + 3956
10. 4549 + 3796
11. 4876 + 2967
12. 7077 + 5946

13. In Holland a car costs £6584. This is £1738 less than the price of the same car in London. How much does the car cost in London?

On this page you will learn to use a standard method for addition.

Examples

$$\begin{array}{r} 1457 \\ +\ \ 928 \\ \hline 2385 \\ \hline {\scriptstyle 1\ \ \ 1} \end{array}$$

$$\begin{array}{r} 2396 \\ +1876 \\ \hline 4272 \\ \hline {\scriptstyle 1\ 1\ 1} \end{array}$$

A

Copy and complete.

1
$$\begin{array}{r} 183 \\ +\ \ 65 \end{array}$$

6
$$\begin{array}{r} 547 \\ +\ \ 54 \end{array}$$

2
$$\begin{array}{r} 456 \\ +\ \ 27 \end{array}$$

7
$$\begin{array}{r} 337 \\ +\ 149 \end{array}$$

3
$$\begin{array}{r} 692 \\ +\ \ 36 \end{array}$$

8
$$\begin{array}{r} 254 \\ +\ 193 \end{array}$$

4
$$\begin{array}{r} 305 \\ +\ \ 78 \end{array}$$

9
$$\begin{array}{r} 529 \\ +\ 256 \end{array}$$

5
$$\begin{array}{r} 761 \\ +\ \ 94 \end{array}$$

10
$$\begin{array}{r} 681 \\ +\ 275 \end{array}$$

11 In one month 384 adults and 65 children stayed at a hotel. How many people stayed at the hotel altogether?

12 In one hour 457 cars were counted passing a school going one way. Only 136 cars were counted going in the other direction. How many cars passed the school altogether?

B

Copy and complete.

1
$$\begin{array}{r} 563 \\ +398 \end{array}$$

6
$$\begin{array}{r} 552 \\ +587 \end{array}$$

2
$$\begin{array}{r} 849 \\ +728 \end{array}$$

7
$$\begin{array}{r} 1785 \\ +\ 369 \end{array}$$

3
$$\begin{array}{r} 695 \\ +563 \end{array}$$

8
$$\begin{array}{r} 1367 \\ +\ 1295 \end{array}$$

4
$$\begin{array}{r} 974 \\ +672 \end{array}$$

9
$$\begin{array}{r} 2948 \\ +\ 727 \end{array}$$

5
$$\begin{array}{r} 781 \\ +368 \end{array}$$

10
$$\begin{array}{r} 4279 \\ +1098 \end{array}$$

11 Jackie's holiday in Tahiti cost £2473. While she was there she spent a further £658. How much did she spend altogether?

C

Set out as in the example.

1 2684 + 1859

2 3967 + 1375

3 5874 + 2687

4 9864 + 3582

5 6497 + 1985

6 8962 + 2479

7 7659 + 2976

8 7586 + 6278

9 6594 + 5257

10 7739 + 4608

11 There were 8552 ants in one anthill and 3949 ants in another. How many ants were there altogether?

12 After flying 4297 miles, a plane landed for refuelling. It flew a further 2635 miles to complete its journey. How far did the plane fly altogether?

13 Louis had £9674 in his bank account. He paid in a further £949. How much did he now have in his account?

On this page you will learn:

- **to add several numbers.**

Example

Add 26, 9, 1326, 154

```
      26    Line-up
       9    the units.
    1326
  + 154
  ────
    1515
     1 2
```

- **to add decimals.**

Example

Add 2·3 m and 160 cm

```
        m
    2·30    Line up the
    1·60    decimal points.
    ────
    3·90
```

A

Copy and complete.

1	2	3	4	5	6
2 43 26 +148	367 13 3485 + 6	1592 341 7 + 53	£ 5·29 4·16 +0·15	£ 3·84 0·61 +0·19	£ 1·97 5·89 +0·46

B

Set out as sums and find the totals.

1 138 + 35 + 2721 + 2 + 79

2 1592 + 341 + 7 + 256 + 53

3 6 + 367 + 13 + 3485 + 458

4 67 + 1816 + 594 + 9 + 182

5 £3·82 + 64p + 9p

6 £4·75 + £1·38 + 7p

7 £6·19 + £1·98 + 27p

8 £8·36 + 27p + 6p

9 2·3 m + 120 cm

10 0·98 m + 156 cm

11 5·8 m + 30 cm

12 1·32 m + 17 cm

C

Set out as sums and find the totals.

1 1752 + 16 + 425 + 5637 + 4

2 9 + 517 + 2743 + 34 + 2841

3 198 + 4915 + 7 + 60 + 1264

4 82 + 343 + 2887 + 6 + 1629

5 126·7 + 8·25 + 1·3

6 6·98 + 13·7 + 0·04

7 14·1 + 1·06 + 0·7

8 2·1 + 15·23 + 138·3

9 1·25 m + 75 cm

10 0·83 m + 6 cm

11 1·9 m + 137 cm + 42 cm

12 21·6 m + 0·37 m + 5 cm

On this page you will learn two informal written methods for subtraction.

COUNTING UP

```
  835                 835
− 267               − 267
───────             ───────
   33  to make 300     33   (300)
  500  to make 800    535   (835)
   35  to make 835    568
───────             ───────
  568
```
or

COMPENSATION

```
  835
− 267
───────
  535   (835 − 300)
+  33   (300 − 267)
───────
  568
```

A

Use both methods for each sum.

1. 351
    − 83

2. 576
    − 64

3. 283
    − 56

4. 697
    − 72

5. 734
    − 97

6. 423
    − 65

7. 345
    − 89

8. 873
    − 57

9. 541
    − 94

10. 860
    − 28

11. Daniel planned to cycle 364 miles in one week. On the first day he cycled 72 miles. How much further did he have to go?

B

Use both methods for each sum.

1. 650
    − 368

2. 314
    − 174

3. 728
    − 291

4. 913
    − 453

5. 585
    − 282

6. 234
    − 185

7. 791
    − 556

8. 518
    − 379

9. 842
    − 259

10. 675
    − 562

11. There are 827 trees in a forest. 236 trees are blown down in a gale. How many trees are left?

12. In January a large store sold 675 television sets. 348 fewer sets were sold in February. How many TVs were sold in February?

C

Set out correctly. Use both methods for each sum.

1. 1491 − 1287
2. 2383 − 1659
3. 4617 − 2434
4. 6174 − 3968
5. 8028 − 4143
6. 3275 − 1839
7. 9812 − 6526
8. 7134 − 2378
9. 4091 − 3754
10. 6726 − 2417
11. 8340 − 5641
12. 5126 − 1751

13. 8340 cars were counted travelling along a motorway in one hour. 5126 cars were going north. How many were going south?

14. In six months Chelsea earned £9163. She saved £2364. How much did she spend?

On this page you will learn to use decomposition.

METHOD 1

$$835 = 800 + 30 + 5 = 800 + 20 + 15 = 700 + 120 + 15$$
$$-267 \quad - 200 + 60 + 7 \quad - 200 + 60 + 7 \quad - 200 + 60 + 7$$
$$500 + 60 + 8 = 568$$

METHOD 2

$$835 = 82^15 = 7^12^15$$
$$-267 \quad -267 \quad -267$$
$$568$$

METHOD 3

$$\overset{7\ 12\ 15}{\cancel{8}\cancel{3}5}$$
$$-267$$
$$568$$

A

Use Method 1.

1   183 − 75   **4**   652 − 86

2   424 − 47   **5**   261 − 53

3   307 − 64   **6**   510 − 72

Use Method 2.

7   748 − 54   **10**   858 − 89

8   960 − 74   **11**   327 − 83

9   592 − 67   **12**   631 − 92

13 A factory made 680 teapots. 52 were broken. How many were not broken?

B

Use Method 2.

1   236 − 172   **4**   625 − 348

2   304 − 185   **5**   947 − 561

3   481 − 213   **6**   530 − 271

Use Method 3.

7   872 − 245   **10**   361 − 289

8   530 − 253   **11**   687 − 431

9   218 − 126   **12**   825 − 367

13 A camp site has room for 275 tents. There are 149 tents on the site. How many more tents can be put up?

14 There are 327 yachts in a Marina. 158 sail out to sea. How many yachts are left?

C

Set out correctly and use Method 3.

1 3274 − 1758

2 4803 − 2645

3 5427 − 2732

4 7621 − 3857

5 6150 − 5692

6 2572 − 1815

7 6083 − 3264

8 3204 − 1753

9 5621 − 3834

10 8347 − 4589

11 7250 − 1087

12 9163 − 2364

13 A library had 4172 books. There were 3238 books on the shelves. How many books had been borrowed?

14 Patrick wants to buy a new car for £9450. he has £6587 in his savings account. How much more money does he need to save?

On this page you will learn:

- to find the difference between numbers with different numbers of digits.

Example

Find the difference between 823 and 1279.

```
  1279   Larger number on top.
–  823   Line up the units.
```

- to find the difference between decimals.

Example

Find the difference between 42·6 and 3·9.

```
  42·6   Line up the
–  3·9   decimal points.
```

A

Copy and complete.

1.
```
  162
–  87
```

2.
```
  231
–  75
```

3.
```
  386
–  54
```

4.
```
  420
–  92
```

5.
```
  758
–  86
```

6.
```
  361
–  47
```

7.
```
  £4·12
– £1·48
```

8.
```
  £3·60
– £1·26
```

9.
```
  £2·94
– £1·75
```

10.
```
  £5·85
– £3·29
```

11.
```
  £3·40
– £2·63
```

12.
```
  £9·36
– £5·79
```

13. Jemima has £7·63 in her purse. She spends £2·48. How much does she have left?

B

Set out correctly and find the differences.

1. 3170 and 364
2. 87 and 4245
3. 128 and 1562
4. 2434 and 79
5. 364 and 1623
6. 7012 and 826
7. £6·24 and £4·38
8. £3·10 and £2·76
9. £8·52 and £3·85
10. 46·3 and 17·5
11. 23·2 and 8·6
12. 2·36 and 1·57

13. A sack of coal contains 46·4 kg. 8·5 kg is removed. How much coal is left?

14. Beth has £7·35. Abbie has £2·69 less. How much does Abbie have?

C

Set out correctly and find the differences.

1. 35 604 and 2913
2. 21 473 and 526
3. 697 and 42 361
4. 1583 and 54 238
5. 43 512 and 2469
6. 748 and 76 150
7. 27·3 and 9·5
8. 13·23 and 1·8
9. 8·5 and 4·76
10. 25·1 and 8·62
11. 2·13 and 0·34
12. 9·32 and 1·9

13. Rayan runs the 200 metres in 22·3 seconds. The winner runs 0·57 seconds faster. What is the winning time?

On this page you will learn to use the inverse relationship of multiplication to division.

Example

Knowing one × or ÷ fact means that you know 3 related facts.

$8 \times 6 = 48$ $6 \times 8 = 48$

$48 \div 6 = 8$ $48 \div 8 = 6$

A

Copy and complete each table.

1

×6	
5 →	30
8 →	
→	24
→	54
7 →	

2

×7	
3 →	21
6 →	
→	63
→	35
8 →	

3

×8	
2 →	16
9 →	
→	40
→	32
8 →	

4

×9	
4 →	36
7 →	
→	81
→	45
8 →	

B

Copy and complete.

1   $\square \times 7 = 63$

2   $6 \times \square = 0$

3   $\square \times 9 = 72$

4   $5 \times \square = 75$

5   $\square \times 8 = 6\cdot4$

6   $\square \times 3 = 27$

7   $0\cdot7 \times \square = 4\cdot2$

8   $\square \times 6 = 48$

9   $7 \times \square = 7\cdot7$

10   $\square \times 1 = 6$

11   $\square \times 6 = 3$

12   $5 \times \square = 100$

13   $\square \times 7 = 4\cdot9$

14   $8 \times \square = 3\cdot2$

15   $\square \times 4 = 360$

Write four different × or ÷ statements for each set of numbers.

16   7, 9, 63

17   54, 9, 6

18   7, 56, 8

19   42, 7, 6

20   120, 6, 20

21   8, 112, 14

22   9, 15, 135

23   96, 8, 12

24   13, 104, 8

25   7, 0·5, 3·5

C

Copy and complete these multiplication squares.

1

×	9	7	10	6
8				
3				
9			90	
7				

2

×		9		8
				64
7	35			
4			24	
				72

3

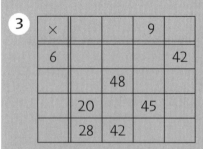

×			9	
6				42
		48		
	20		45	
	28	42		

4

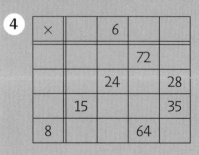

×		6		
			72	
		24		28
	15			35
8		64		

On this page you will learn to use the vocabulary of multiplication.

A

Write a number sentence for each problem and work out the answer.

1 What is 8 times 5?

2 Multiply 6 by 3.

3 Find 9 lots of 4.

4 What is 6 times greater than 20?

5 Find the product of 5 and 7.

6 What is 11 multiplied by 8?

7 A tree is 7 m tall. A block of flats is 6 times higher. How tall is the block of flats?

8 There are 20 CDs in each tray. There are 5 trays. How many CDs are there?

9 Aster has 16 marbles. Sheree has five times as many. How many marbles does Sheree have?

10 A small box holds 80 tea bags. A larger box holds twice as many. How many tea bags does the larger box hold?

B

Write a number sentence for each problem and work out the answer.

1 What is 7 times 8?

2 Find the product of 21 and 7.

3 What is 30 multiplied by 15?

4 What is 10 times greater than 0·7?

5 There are 52 playing cards in a pack. How many cards are there in 4 packs?

6 A model of a bridge is 60 cm long. The bridge is 50 times longer. How long is the bridge in metres?

7 There are 12 rubbers in a box. There are 6 boxes. How many rubbers are there altogether?

8 9 boys are members of a gymnastic club. There are 7 times as many girl members. How many members are there altogether?

C

1 Look at the numbers in the box.

5	6	7	8	9

   a) What is the largest number multiplied by the smallest number?

   b) Find the square of the sum of the even numbers.

   c) Find the sum of the two smallest numbers. Multiply this number by their product.

   d) Find the product of the four smallest numbers.

   e) Multiply the smallest number by the total of all five numbers.

   f) Find all the different products you can make by using three of the numbers.

2 There are 16 flowers in each tray. How many flowers are there in 9 trays?

3 A concrete slab weighs 7·5 kg. What do eight slabs weigh?

4 How many days are there in 13 weeks?

5 Javed earns £800 each month. How much does he earn in a year?

On this page you will practise the multiplication and division facts.

A

Write the answers only.

1	3×2	**25**	$21 \div 3$
2	8×2	**26**	$15 \div 3$
3	9×2	**27**	$18 \div 3$
4	0×2	**28**	$24 \div 3$
5	7×2	**29**	$9 \div 3$
6	6×2	**30**	$27 \div 3$
7	10×3	**31**	$45 \div 5$
8	6×3	**32**	$20 \div 5$
9	7×3	**33**	$35 \div 5$
10	9×3	**34**	$50 \div 5$
11	4×3	**35**	$25 \div 5$
12	8×3	**36**	$40 \div 5$
13	5×4	**37**	$60 \div 10$
14	7×4	**38**	$80 \div 10$
15	9×4	**39**	$40 \div 10$
16	6×4	**40**	$70 \div 10$
17	1×4	**41**	$100 \div 10$
18	8×4	**42**	$90 \div 10$
19	6×5	**43**	$36 \div 4$
20	8×5	**44**	$24 \div 4$
21	5×5	**45**	$16 \div 4$
22	3×5	**46**	$32 \div 4$
23	10×5	**47**	$40 \div 4$
24	7×5	**48**	$28 \div 4$

49 Copy and complete the multiplication square.

×	9	3	7
6			
8			
4			

B

Copy and complete each of the tables.

1

×6
4 → 24
8 →
6 →
1 →
→ 30
→ 0
→ 42
→ 54

2

×7
6 → 42
0 →
7 →
9 →
→ 56
→ 28
→ 7
→ 35

3

×8
8 → 64
0 →
5 →
4 →
→ 8
→ 48
→ 72
→ 56

4

×9
5 → 45
7 →
9 →
10 →
→ 36
→ 72
→ 0
→ 54

C

Write the answers only.

1	9×0.6	**11**	$4.5 \div 9$
2	6×0.8	**12**	$3.2 \div 4$
3	0.5×7	**13**	$4.9 \div 7$
4	6×9	**14**	$72 \div 8$
5	0.5×0.8	**15**	$6.3 \div 7$
6	7×6	**16**	$42 \div 6$
7	0.8×8	**17**	$5.6 \div 8$
8	8×0.7	**18**	$3.0 \div 6$
9	7×4	**19**	$4.2 \div 7$
10	0.8×6	**20**	$5.4 \div 9$

Copy and complete.

21 $\square \times 4 = 3.6$

22 $8 \times \square = 40$

23 $\square \div 9 = 0.8$

24 $6.3 \div \square = 0.9$

25 $\square \times 9 = 4.5$

26 $20 \times \square = 400$

27 $\square \div 6 = 8$

28 $6.4 \div \square = 0.8$

29 $\square \times 7 = 56$

30 $5 \times \square = 3.5$

31 $\square \div 7 = 0.7$

32 $42 \div \square = 7$

33 $\square \times 8 = 7.2$

34 $0.7 \times \square = 2.8$

35 $\square \div 3 = 0.8$

36 $8.1 \div \square = 0.9$

On this page you will learn to use the inverse relationship of division to multiplication.

Example   Knowing one × or ÷ fact means that you know 3 related facts.

$90 \div 6 = 15$ $90 \div 15 = 6$

$15 \times 6 = 90$ $6 \times 15 = 90$

A

Copy and complete the tables.

1

÷6
30 → 5
54 →
→ 6
24 →
48 →
→ 7

2

÷7
21 → 3
56 →
→ 5
→ 9
28 →
49 →

3

÷8
16 → 2
64 →
→ 7
24 →
→ 9
→ 6

4

÷9
90 → 10
36 →
→ 9
18 →
54 →
→ 8

B

Copy and complete.

1 $81 \div \square = 9$

2 $77 \div \square = 7$

3 $5 \div \square = 0.5$

4 $\square \div 8 = 6$

5 $\square \div 6 = 7$

6 $54 \div \square = 6$

7 $120 \div \square = 6$

8 $14 \div \square = 14$

9 $\square \div 8 = 25$

10 $\square \div 5 = 9$

11 $100 \div \square = 5$

12 $24 \div \square = 2.4$

13 $80 \div \square = 20$

14 $\square \div 10 = 8.5$

15 $\square \div 1 = 8$

16 $500 \div \square = 10$

17 $30 \div \square = 2$

18 $15 \div \square = 1.5$

19 $\square \div 15 = 8$

20 $\square \div 12 = 6$

For each statement write three related × or ÷ statements.

21 $72 \div 12 = 6$

22 $5 \times 15 = 75$

23 $96 \div 6 = 16$

24 $21 \times 8 = 168$

25 $7 \times 19 = 133$

C

Copy and complete the tables.

1

Input		Output
7·2	÷9	
300	÷15	
	÷7	30
	÷1	0·8
	÷8	0·5
60		0·6
92		9·2
11		11

2

Input		Output
3	÷100	
4·8	÷6	
25	÷10	
	÷7	0·8
	÷4	2·5
7·2		0·9
4		0·04
320		40

3

Input		Output
75	÷1	
500	÷20	
6	÷12	
	÷9	9
	÷9	0·9
13		0·13
6·3		0·9
10		0·25

4 What number, when divided by 9 and then multiplied by 12, gives an answer of 60?

On this page you will learn to use the vocabulary of division.

A

Write a number sentence for each problem and work out the answer.

1. Divide 27 by 3.

2. Share 60 by 10.

3. How many 4s make 28?

4. What is 24 divided by 8?

5. What is 45 shared by 9?

6. How many groups of 2 make 50?

7. How many 6-a-side teams can be made from 36 children?

8. Share 48 stickers between 4 children.

9. How many weeks are there in 63 days?

10. Tariq's father is 54. Tariq is one third of his age. How old is Tariq?

11. One fifth of the flowers in a garden are roses. There are 100 flowers in the garden. How many are roses?

12. Ten footballs cost £150. What is the cost of one football?

B

Write a number sentence for each problem and work out the answer.

1. Envelopes are sold in packets of 50. How many packets can be made from 600 envelopes?

2. A van can carry 15 crates. How many journeys are necessary to carry 120 crates?

3. Concert tickets cost £7·50. How many tickets can be bought for £90·00?

4. 8 tins of rhubarb weigh 3200 g. How much does each tin weigh?

5. Jenny has 60 marbles. One third of her marbles are yellow and one quarter are red. How many marbles are a different colour?

6. Six friends share the cost of a meal equally between them. The meal costs £75. How much should each person pay?

C

Write a number sentence for each problem and work out the answer.

1. There are 24 olives in each jar. How many jars can be filled from 360 olives?

2. 450 cm of wood is cut into 25 equal lengths. How long is each length of wood?

3. The 336 children in a school are divided into 4 equal teams. How many children are in each team?

4. 9 cans of cola cost £7·20. What is the price of one can?

5. What is one eighth of £100?

6. Six people can sit at each table. How many tables are needed for 330 people?

7. Five hundred raffle tickets are sold. One in every twenty tickets wins a prize. How many prizes are needed?

On this page you will learn:

- to give a remainder as a fraction.
- to give a remainder as a decimal.

Examples

$77 \div 4 = 19\frac{1}{4}$ (This is a mixed fraction.)

Examples

£77 ÷ 4 = £19·25, because £1 ÷ 4 = £0·25.

£53 ÷ 10 = £5·30, because £3 ÷ 10 = £0·30.

A

Give the answer as a mixed fraction.

1. $33 \div 2$
2. $73 \div 5$
3. $19 \div 3$
4. $137 \div 10$
5. $27 \div 4$
6. $21 \div 2$
7. $33 \div 5$
8. $37 \div 4$
9. $23 \div 3$
10. $62 \div 5$

Give the answer as a decimal.

11. £17 ÷ 2
12. £77 ÷ 10
13. £29 ÷ 4
14. £28 ÷ 5
15. £23 ÷ 4
16. £27 ÷ 2
17. £19 ÷ 4
18. £57 ÷ 5
19. £12 ÷ 10
20. £39 ÷ 5

21. A rope is 31 metres long. It is cut in half. How long is each length in metres?

22. Five people share a prize of £17. How much should each person receive?

23. Two friends share the cost of a meal. The bill is £23. How much should each person pay?

B

Give the answer as a mixed fraction.

1. $83 \div 4$
2. $39 \div 7$
3. $73 \div 9$
4. $38 \div 6$
5. $136 \div 25$
6. $109 \div 5$
7. $43 \div 8$
8. $173 \div 10$
9. $641 \div 100$
10. $26 \div 7$

Give the answer as a decimal.

11. $47 \div 2$
12. $127 \div 4$
13. $131 \div 5$
14. $427 \div 10$
15. $93 \div 4$
16. £4·80 ÷ 3
17. £9·20 ÷ 4
18. £12·00 ÷ 5
19. £9·10 ÷ 2
20. £8·10 ÷ 6

21. A CD player costs £76. The price is reduced by one tenth. What is the new price?

22. It takes 115 litres of water to fill four identical fish tanks. How much water does each tank hold?

C

Copy and complete.

1. $\square \div 7 = 12\frac{2}{7}$
2. $\square \div 8 = 4\frac{7}{8}$
3. $\square \div 9 = 8\frac{1}{9}$
4. $\square \div 6 = 15\frac{5}{6}$
5. $\square \div 100 = 14\frac{91}{100}$
6. $\square \div 6 = 26\frac{1}{6}$
7. $\square \div 10 = 16\frac{7}{10}$
8. $\square \div 9 = 19\frac{1}{9}$
9. $\square \div 8 = 16\frac{3}{8}$
10. $\square \div 7 = 17\frac{1}{7}$
11. $\square \div 4 = 83\frac{3}{4}$
12. $\square \div 12 = 8\frac{5}{12}$

Give the answer as a decimal fraction. If necessary round off to one decimal place.

13. $94 \div 4$
14. $137 \div 10$
15. $94 \div 5$
16. $90 \div 7$
17. $52 \div 3$
18. $111 \div 9$
19. $79 \div 5$
20. $87 \div 6$
21. $100 \div 6$
22. $122 \div 7$

On this page you will learn to make sensible decisions about rounding up or down after division.

Examples

How many £6 tickets can I buy with £87?

$87 \div 6 = 14$ remainder 3

Answer   14 tickets can be bought.

An egg box holds 6 eggs.
How many boxes do I need to hold 87 eggs?

$87 \div 6 = 14$ remainder 3

Answer   15 boxes are needed.

Yoghurts are sold in packs of four.
How many packs can be made from 50 yoghurts?

$50 \div 4 = 12$ remainder 2

Answer   12 packs can be made.

Kyle saves £4 each week. How many weeks will it take him to save £50?

$50 \div 4 = 12$ remainder 2

Answer   It takes 13 weeks.

A

1. One lorry can carry 8 containers. How many lorries are needed to carry 55 containers?

2. There are 40 straws in each packet. How many packets can be made up from 300 straws?

3. An egg box holds 6 eggs. How many boxes can be filled with 40 eggs?

4. A car can carry 3 children as passengers. How many cars are needed to carry 40 children?

5. How many teams of 4 can be made from a class of 31 children?

6. Jennifer saves 30p every day. How many days will it take her to save £2?

7. 10 CDs can be stored in a rack. How many racks are needed to store 123 CDs?

8. A train fare is £5. How many tickets can be bought for £78?

9. For a fancy dress costume Natalie needs ribbons which are 80 cm long. How many can she cut from 5 metres of ribbon?

10. 8 children can sleep in a large tent. How many tents are needed for 60 children?

B

1. There are beds for 14 patients in each ward of a hospital. How many wards are needed for 90 patients?

2. There are 80 drawing pins in each box. How many boxes can be filled from 1000 drawing pins?

3. Video tapes are sold in packs of 8. How many packs can be made from 142 tapes?

4. Safraz wants to buy a bicycle which costs £200. He saves £15 each week. How many weeks will it take to save the £200 he needs?

5. A coach trip party stops at a cafe where the teas cost 60p. How many teas can be bought for £20?

6. Apples are packed in boxes of 20. How many boxes are needed to store 450 apples?

7. How many 6-a-side football teams can be made up from 83 players?

8. The tables at a wedding reception seat 12 people. There are 100 guests. How many tables are needed?

9. There are 40 beads in a necklace. How many necklaces can be made from 350 beads?

10. A whole school is planning a trip to London. One coach can carry 52 passengers. How many coaches are needed to carry all 340 passengers?

C

1. Cough sweets are sold in packets of 12. How many packets can be made up from 200 sweets?

2. Each money bag holds 30 coins. How many bags are needed for 1000 coins?

3. How many 11-a-side football teams can be made up from 140 players?

4. A garden centre can fit 8 plants on each tray. How many trays are needed to display 260 plants?

5. Hayley saves £25 each month towards her holiday. How many weeks will it take her to save the £140 she needs?

6. A loaf of bread has 22 slices. A cafe needs 300 slices of bread for sandwiches. How many loaves does the cafe owner need to buy?

7. A village hall can fit 24 chairs into one row. How many rows are needed to seat 300 people?

8. Pencils are packed into boxes of 15. How many boxes can be filled with 265 pencils?

9. A car transporter can carry 12 cars. How many transporters are needed to carry 340 cars?

10. Cakes cost 45p. How many can be bought for £12?

On this page you will learn to use factors to multiply and divide.

Examples

$$15 \times 6 = (15 \times 3) \times 2$$
$$= 45 \times 2$$
$$= 90$$

$$90 \div 6 = (90 \div 3) \div 2$$
$$= 30 \div 2$$
$$= 15$$

 A

Copy and complete.

1. $7 \times 6 = 7 \times 3 \times 2 = \square \times 2 =$
2. $9 \times 8 = 9 \times 4 \times 2 = \square \times 2 =$
3. $11 \times 12 = 11 \times 6 \times 2 = \square \times 2 =$
4. $9 \times 6 = 9 \times 3 \times 2 = \square \times 2 =$
5. $7 \times 8 = 7 \times 4 \times 2 = \square \times 2 =$
6. $63 \div 9 = 63 \div 3 \div 3 = \square \div 3 =$
7. $84 \div 6 = 84 \div 2 \div 3 = \square \div 3 =$
8. $72 \div 12 = 72 \div 2 \div 6 = \square \div 6 =$
9. $64 \div 8 = 64 \div 2 \div 4 = \square \div 4 =$
10. $48 \div 16 = 48 \div 2 \div 8 = \square \div 8 =$

B

Use factors to work out:

1. 15×6
2. 12×8
3. 13×12
4. $128 \div 8$
5. $180 \div 12$
6. $189 \div 9$
7. 9×14
8. 17×9
9. $120 \div 15$
10. $210 \div 14$

C

Use factors to work out:

1. 13×16
2. 25×18
3. 17×21
4. 13×24
5. 9×27
6. $189 \div 21$
7. $288 \div 16$
8. $306 \div 18$
9. $240 \div 16$
10. $255 \div 15$

Now you will learn to work out a times-table by adding.

Example

FOURS	4	8	12	16	20	24	28	32	36	40
TENS	10	20	30	40	50	60	70	80	90	100
FOURTEENS	14	28	42	56	70	84	98	112	126	140

 A

Copy and complete the table to work out the 8 times-table.

THREES	3	6	9	12						30
FIVES	5	10	15							
EIGHTS	8	16								

B

Copy and continue to ×10.

TWOS	TENS	TWELVES
2	10	12
4	20	24

C

Copy and continue to ×10.

SEVENS	TENS	SEVENTEENS
7	10	17
14	20	34

On this page you will learn to multiply a number by 19 or 21.

Examples $14 \times 21 = (14 \times 20) + (14 \times 1)$ $14 \times 19 = (14 \times 20) - (14 \times 1)$

$= 280 + 14$ $= 280 - 14$

$= 294$ $= 266$

A

Work out

1. 14×9
2. 16×9
3. 13×9
4. 11×11
5. 14×11
6. 18×11
7. 17×9
8. 19×9
9. 22×9
10. 16×11

B

Work out

1. 8×19
2. 12×19
3. 15×19
4. 7×21
5. 11×21
6. 16×21
7. 17×19
8. 22×19
9. 26×19
10. 18×21

11. 23×21
12. 21×21
13. 13×19
14. 24×19
15. 19×19
16. 28×19
17. 14×21
18. 27×21
19. 19×21
20. 24×21

C

Copy and complete.

1. $\square \div 49 = 13$
2. $\square \div 51 = 12$
3. $\square \div 99 = 11$
4. $\square \div 101 = 14$
5. $\square \div 49 = 16$
6. $\square \div 51 = 15$
7. $\square \div 99 = 15$
8. $\square \div 101 = 16$
9. $\square \div 49 = 18$
10. $\square \div 51 = 19$

Now you will learn to multiply by partitioning.

Examples $53 \times 6 = (50 \times 6) + (3 \times 6)$ $29 \times 5 = (20 \times 5) + (9 \times 5)$

$= 300 + 18$ $= 100 + 45$

$= 318$ $= 145$

A

Work out

1. $13 \times 3 = (10 \times 3) + (3 \times 3) =$
2. $18 \times 3 = (10 \times 3) + (8 \times 3) =$
3. $24 \times 3 = (20 \times 3) + (4 \times 3) =$
4. $12 \times 4 = (10 \times 4) + (2 \times 4) =$
5. $19 \times 4 = (10 \times 4) + (9 \times 4) =$
6. $23 \times 4 = (20 \times 4) + (3 \times 4) =$
7. $29 \times 3 = (20 \times 3) + (9 \times 3) =$
8. $32 \times 3 = (30 \times 3) + (2 \times 3) =$
9. $28 \times 4 = (20 \times 4) + (8 \times 4) =$
10. $33 \times 4 = (30 \times 4) + (3 \times 4) =$

B

Work out

1. 34×4
2. 57×5
3. 42×6
4. 24×7
5. 28×8
6. 32×9
7. 47×4
8. 38×5
9. 56×6
10. 35×7

C

Copy and complete

1. $\square \div 6 = 62$
2. $\square \div 7 = 86$
3. $\square \div 7 = 73$
4. $\square \div 8 = 59$
5. $\square \div 8 = 84$
6. $\square \div 9 = 86$
7. $\square \div 6 = 7 \cdot 5$
8. $\square \div 7 = 5 \cdot 8$
9. $\square \div 6 = 6 \cdot 7$
10. $\square \div 8 = 9 \cdot 2$

On this page you will practise:

- multiplying a multiple of 10 by a multiple of 100.

- dividing a multiple of 100 by 10, 100 or 1000.

Examples

$50 \times 200 = 10\,000$ $70 \times 600 = 42\,000$

Examples

$6400 \div 100 = 64$ $2000 \div 1000 = 2$

A

Multiply by 10.

1	35	**5**	269
2	52	**6**	386
3	81	**7**	67
4	174	**8**	290

Divide by 10.

9	2000	**13**	3000
10	400	**14**	5000
11	7000	**15**	600
12	800	**16**	9000

Multiply by 100.

17	27	**21**	51
18	64	**22**	8
19	7	**23**	90
20	46	**24**	38

Divide by 100.

25	6000	**29**	4000
26	200	**30**	8000
27	1000	**31**	300
28	900	**32**	7000

B

Work out

1	60×200
2	70×300
3	30×400
4	70×500
5	30×800
6	40×900
7	60×500
8	40×700
9	$3000 \div 10$
10	$5800 \div 100$
11	$4000 \div 1000$
12	$6200 \div 10$
13	$9000 \div 100$
14	$5000 \div 1000$
15	$7600 \div 10$
16	$3000 \div 1000$

Copy and complete.

17	$60 \times \square = 48\,000$
18	$2700 \div \square = 27$
19	$\square \times 600 = 54\,000$
20	$\square \div 1000 = 9$
21	$\square \times 600 = 24\,000$
22	$4300 \div \square = 430$
23	$60 \times \square = 42\,000$
24	$\square \div 100 = 89$

C

Copy and complete the tables.

1
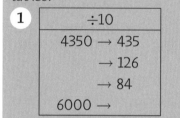

÷10	
4350	→ 435
	→ 126
	→ 84
6000	→

2
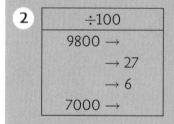

÷100	
9800	→
	→ 27
	→ 6
7000	→

3
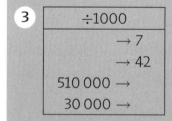

÷1000	
	→ 7
	→ 42
510 000	→
30 000	→

4
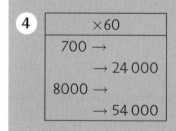

×60	
700	→
	→ 24 000
8000	→
	→ 54 000

5
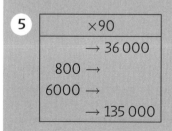

×90	
	→ 36 000
800	→
6000	→
	→ 135 000

On this page you will practise:

- doubling multiples of 5.
- halving multiples of 10.

Example

$145 \times 2 = (100 \times 2) + (40 \times 2) + (5 \times 2)$
$= 200 + 80 + 10$
$= 290$

Example

$570 \div 2 = (500 \div 2) + (70 \div 2)$
$= 250 + 35$
$= 285$

A

Double these numbers.

1	15	**9**	30
2	20	**10**	55
3	40	**11**	35
4	25	**12**	80
5	45	**13**	110
6	60	**14**	90
7	95	**15**	75
8	65	**16**	130

Halve these numbers.

17	80	**25**	100
18	110	**26**	140
19	150	**27**	130
20	70	**28**	190
21	170	**29**	200
22	120	**30**	280
23	180	**31**	160
24	90	**32**	250

33 The postbox is 270 metres from Lauren's house. How far does she walk when she posts a letter?

34 How many pairs can be made from 500 socks?

B

Write the answers only.

1	270×2	**7**	$270 \div 2$
2	335×2	**8**	$330 \div 2$
3	175×2	**9**	$490 \div 2$
4	255×2	**10**	$720 \div 2$
5	360×2	**11**	$850 \div 2$
6	485×2	**12**	$510 \div 2$

Copy and complete.

13 $\square \times 2 = 150$

14 $\square \div 2 = 145$

15 $\square \times 2 = 530$

16 $\square \div 2 = 290$

17 $\square \times 2 = 590$

18 $\square \div 2 = 275$

19 $\square \times 2 = 950$

20 $\square \div 2 = 355$

21 $\square \times 2 = 780$

22 $\square \div 2 = 335$

23 $\square \times 2 = 370$

24 $\square \div 2 = 165$

25 A prize of £560 is shared equally between the two winners. How much should each person receive?

C

Copy and complete the tables.

1

Double
$95 \rightarrow 190$
$445 \rightarrow$
$640 \rightarrow$
$785 \rightarrow$
$970 \rightarrow$
$\rightarrow 830$
$\rightarrow 1380$
$\rightarrow 1750$
$\rightarrow 1890$

2

Halve
$750 \rightarrow 375$
$870 \rightarrow$
$1560 \rightarrow$
$1630 \rightarrow$
$1790 \rightarrow$
$\rightarrow 235$
$\rightarrow 490$
$\rightarrow 860$
$\rightarrow 775$

3 512 is the 10th number in the sequence 1, 2, 4, 8 …

a) What is the 12th number in the sequence?

b) What is the 9th number?

On this page you will practise:

- multiplying a multiple of 10 or 100 by a single-digit number.

- multiplying a two-digit number by a single-digit number.

Examples

$40 \times 9 = 360$ $500 \times 7 = 3500$

Example

$28 \times 4 = (20 \times 4) + (8 \times 4) = 80 + 32 = 112$

A

Work out.

1. 80×2
2. 90×3
3. 50×8
4. 90×5

5. 20×6
6. 80×10
7. 30×7
8. 80×4

9. 30×9
10. 70×10
11. 60×5
12. 40×6

13. 18×2
14. 14×3
15. 15×5
16. 13×4

17. 19×3
18. 36×2
19. 19×5
20. 17×4

21. 27×2
22. 25×3
23. 24×5
24. 23×4

B

Copy and complete.

1. $70 \times 5 = \square$
2. $600 \times 7 = \square$
3. $60 \times 4 = \square$
4. $800 \times 3 = \square$

5. $48 \times 9 = \square$
6. $32 \times 7 = \square$
7. $54 \times 5 = \square$
8. $24 \times 8 = \square$

9. $70 \times \square = 420$
10. $800 \times \square = 7200$
11. $60 \times \square = 480$
12. $600 \times \square = 3600$

13. $34 \times \square = 170$
14. $28 \times \square = 112$
15. $52 \times \square = 468$
16. $43 \times \square = 258$

17. $\square \times 5 = 4000$
18. $\square \times 2 = 140$
19. $\square \times 4 = 3600$
20. $\square \times 6 = 540$

21. $\square \times 3 = 108$
22. $\square \times 6 = 78$
23. $\square \times 5 = 165$
24. $\square \times 4 = 88$

C

Copy and complete the tables.

1

×6	
700	→ 4200
6000	→
87	→
	→ 48 000
	→ 3600
	→ 378
79	→
	→ 54 000
54	→

3

×8	
6000	→
94	→
79	→
	→ 5600
	→ 72 000
	→ 288
800	→
67	→
	→ 32 000

2

×7	
8000	→ 56 000
79	→
66	→
	→ 49 000
600	→
	→ 385
	→ 6300
98	→
	→ 35 000

4

×9	
9000	→ 81 000
49	→
57	→
	→ 54 000
700	→
	→ 765
	→ 4500
78	→
	→ 72 000

5. In six months Robert saves £2400. How much does he save each month?

6. Forty-six screws are needed to make one wardrobe. How many screws are needed to make eight wardrobes?

7. Each day a plane is flown 9000 miles. How far is it flown in one week?

On this page you will practise doubling and halving and learn to use partitioning to double and halve.

Examples

Double 58 = (50 × 2) + (8 × 2) = 100 + 16 = 116

Half of 358 = (300 ÷ 2) + (50 ÷ 2) + (8 ÷ 2) = 150 + 25 + 4 = 179

A

Double each number.

1 35	**5** 18	**9** 280
2 23	**6** 36	**10** 3100
3 47	**7** 440	**11** 2700
4 42	**8** 390	**12** 4900

Halve each number.

13 34	**17** 98	**21** 760
14 46	**18** 58	**22** 3600
15 74	**19** 880	**23** 9600
16 52	**20** 940	**24** 7800

Copy and complete.

25 Double 42 = (40 × 2) + (2 × 2) =

26 Double 57 = (50 × 2) + (7 × 2) =

27 Double 86 = (80 × 2) + (6 × 2) =

28 Double 48 = (40 × 2) + (8 × 2) =

29 Double 64 = (60 × 2) + (4 × 2) =

30 Double 73 = (70 × 2) + (3 × 2) =

31 Double 98 = (90 × 2) + (8 × 2) =

32 Double 79 = (70 × 2) + (9 × 2) =

Copy and complete to find half of:

33 184 (100 ÷ 2) + (80 ÷ 2) + (4 ÷ 2) =

34 112 (100 ÷ 2) + (10 ÷ 2) + (2 ÷ 2) =

35 176 (100 ÷ 2) + (70 ÷ 2) + (6 ÷ 2) =

36 158 (100 ÷ 2) + (50 ÷ 2) + (8 ÷ 2) =

37 194 (100 ÷ 2) + (90 ÷ 2) + (4 ÷ 2) =

38 164 (100 ÷ 2) + (60 ÷ 2) + (4 ÷ 2) =

39 138 (100 ÷ 2) + (30 ÷ 2) + (8 ÷ 2) =

40 172 (100 ÷ 2) + (70 ÷ 2) + (2 ÷ 2) =

B

Write the answer only.

1 52 × 2

2 67 × 2

3 59 × 2

4 65 × 2

5 840 × 2

6 7600 × 2

7 870 × 2

8 9300 × 2

9 92 ÷ 2

10 84 ÷ 2

11 116 ÷ 2

12 162 ÷ 2

13 560 ÷ 2

14 1580 ÷ 2

15 12 800 ÷ 2

16 19 600 ÷ 2

Work out by partitioning.

17 162 × 2

18 137 × 2

19 86 × 2

20 135 × 2

21 218 ÷ 2

22 354 ÷ 2

23 236 ÷ 2

24 342 ÷ 2

C

Copy and complete.

1 ☐ × 2 = 1460

2 ☐ × 2 = 1940

3 ☐ × 2 = 1380

4 ☐ × 2 = 152

5 ☐ ÷ 2 = 550

6 ☐ ÷ 2 = 660

7 ☐ ÷ 2 = 970

8 ☐ ÷ 2 = 8300

9 ☐ × 2 = 11 600

10 ☐ × 2 = 19 800

11 ☐ × 2 = 12·4

12 ☐ × 2 = 16·8

13 ☐ ÷ 2 = 6900

14 ☐ ÷ 2 = 7800

15 ☐ ÷ 2 = 7·4

16 ☐ ÷ 2 = 3·7

17 ☐ × 2 = 19·6

18 ☐ × 2 = 1·8

19 ☐ × 2 = 1·12

20 ☐ × 2 = 1·5

21 ☐ ÷ 2 = 8·9

22 ☐ ÷ 2 = 0·62

23 ☐ ÷ 2 = 0·48

24 ☐ ÷ 2 = 0·76

On this page you will learn to use doubling or halving to solve calculations.

Examples

MULTIPLICATION

$16 \times 5 = (16 \times 10) \div 2 = 160 \div 2 = 80$

$36 \times 50 = (36 \times 100) \div 2$
$\qquad = 3600 \div 2 = 1800$

$16 \times 53 = (8 \times 53) \times 2 = 424 \times 2 = 848$

$45 \times 14 = 90 \times 7 = 630$

FRACTIONS

Find $\frac{1}{12}$ of 24.   Find $\frac{1}{20}$ of 30.

$\frac{1}{3}$ of 24 = 8 $\frac{1}{10}$ of 30 = 3

$\frac{1}{6}$ of 24 = 4 $\frac{1}{20}$ of 30 = 1·5

$\frac{1}{12}$ of 24 = 2

MULTIPLES

Some multiples of 12 can be worked out by doubling.

$1 \times 12 = 12$
$2 \times 12 = 24$
$4 \times 12 = 48$
$8 \times 12 = 96$
$16 \times 12 = 192$

These multiples can be used to solve calculations.

$17 \times 12 = (16 \times 12) + (1 \times 12)$
$\qquad = 192 + 12$
$\qquad = 204$

$23 \times 12 = (16 \times 12) + (8 \times 12) - (1 \times 12)$
$\qquad = 192 + 96 - 12$
$\qquad = 276$

$13 \times 12 = (8 \times 12) + (4 \times 12) + (1 \times 12)$
$\qquad = 96 + 48 + 12$
$\qquad = 156$

A

Make the 12 times-table by doubling the 6 times-table.

1

6 times-table	12 times-table
6	12
12	
18	
24	
30	60
36	
42	
48	
54	
60	

Work out by doubling or halving.
Show the method used.

2 17×4 **6** 38×5 **10** 24×20

3 26×4 **7** 64×5 **11** 27×20

4 33×4 **8** 14×20 **12** 42×4

5 42×5 **9** 17×20 **13** 88×5

Work out by doubling.

14 $1 \times 15 = \square$ **15** $1 \times 14 = \square$

$\quad 2 \times 15 = \square$ $\quad 2 \times 14 = \square$

$\quad 4 \times 15 = \square$ $\quad 4 \times 14 = \square$

$\quad 8 \times 15 = \square$ $\quad 8 \times 14 = \square$

$\quad 16 \times 15 = \square$ $\quad 16 \times 14 = \square$

Use halving to solve.

16 $\frac{1}{2}$ of 64 = $\square$ **17** $\frac{1}{3}$ of 60 = $\square$

$\quad \frac{1}{4}$ of 64 = $\square$ $\quad \frac{1}{6}$ of 60 = $\square$

$\quad \frac{1}{8}$ of 64 = $\square$ $\quad \frac{1}{12}$ of 60 = $\square$

B

Make the 14 times-table by doubling the 7 times-table.

1

7 times-table	14 times-table
7	14
14	
21	
28	
35	
42	
49	
56	
63	
70	140

Work out by doubling or halving. Show the method used.

2 18×5 **7** 83×50 **12** 26×12

3 24×5 **8** 67×50 **13** 14×35

4 46×5 **9** 17×16 **14** 16×25

5 41×50 **10** 13×14 **15** 12×45

6 36×50 **11** 41×18 **16** 32×15

By doubling, work out multiples of 21 to 16×21 as in the example on page 60. Use your multiples to work out:

17 15×21 **19** 19×21 **21** 23×21

18 12×21 **20** 14×21 **22** 26×21

Work out both problems. Use halving to solve the second problem of each pair.

23 $\frac{1}{3}$ of 900   **27** $\frac{1}{10}$ of 700
$\frac{1}{6}$ of 900 $\frac{1}{20}$ of 700

24 $\frac{1}{3}$ of 27   **28** $\frac{1}{10}$ of 42
$\frac{1}{6}$ of 27 $\frac{1}{20}$ of 42

25 $\frac{1}{3}$ of 540   **29** $\frac{1}{10}$ of 250
$\frac{1}{6}$ of 540 $\frac{1}{20}$ of 250

26 $\frac{1}{3}$ of 99   **30** $\frac{1}{10}$ of 380
$\frac{1}{6}$ of 99 $\frac{1}{20}$ of 380

C

Work out by doubling or halving. Show the method used.

1 14×55 **7** 14×39

2 65×12 **8** 47×12

3 24×35 **9** 36×25

4 38×45 **10** 18×25

5 16×23 **11** 26×25

6 27×18 **12** 54×25

By doubling, work out multiples of 16 to 16×16. Use them to work out:

13 7×16 **16** 22×16

14 13×16 **17** 31×16

15 19×16 **18** 28×16.

Copy and complete. Use halving to solve the second and third problems.

19 $\frac{1}{3}$ of 180   **22** $\frac{1}{3}$ of 9
$\frac{1}{6}$ of 180 $\frac{1}{6}$ of 9
$\frac{1}{12}$ of 180 $\frac{1}{12}$ of 9

20 $\frac{1}{3}$ of 66   **23** $\frac{1}{3}$ of 15
$\frac{1}{6}$ of 66 $\frac{1}{6}$ of 15
$\frac{1}{12}$ of 66 $\frac{1}{12}$ of 15

21 $\frac{1}{3}$ of 3000   **24** $\frac{1}{3}$ of 75
$\frac{1}{6}$ of 3000 $\frac{1}{6}$ of 75
$\frac{1}{12}$ of 3000 $\frac{1}{12}$ of 75

Copy and complete. Use halving to solve the second problem.

25 $\frac{1}{10}$ of 430   **28** $\frac{1}{10}$ of 0·6
$\frac{1}{20}$ of 430 $\frac{1}{20}$ of 0·6

26 $\frac{1}{10}$ of 90   **29** $\frac{1}{10}$ of 27
$\frac{1}{20}$ of 90 $\frac{1}{20}$ of 27

27 $\frac{1}{10}$ of 35   **30** $\frac{1}{10}$ of 1
$\frac{1}{20}$ of 35 $\frac{1}{20}$ of 1

On this page you will learn the grid method for multiplication.

Example 1

235×7

$\times$	200	30	5
7	1400	210	35

$= 1645$

Example 2

64×27

$\times$	60	4
20	1200	80
7	420	28

```
  1280
+  448
  1728
```

A

Copy and complete.

1

$\times$	30	9
3		

$=$

2

$\times$	50	8
2		

$=$

3

$\times$	10	7
6		

$=$

4

$\times$	30	6
4		

$=$

5

$\times$	10	4
8		

$=$

6

$\times$	20	8
5		

$=$

7

$\times$	20	3
6		

$=$

8

$\times$	10	5
7		

$=$

Use the grid method.

9 25×8 **13** 19×8

10 42×9 **14** 45×6

11 43×7 **15** 87×3

12 58×4 **16** 35×7

B

Copy and complete.

1

$\times$	200	40	3
6			

$=$

2

$\times$	300	70	5
7			

$=$

Use the grid method.

3 168×9 **5** 698×5

4 429×8 **6** 547×4

Copy and complete.

7

$\times$	40	3
20		
8		

$=$

8

$\times$	50	3
30		
2		

$=$

9

$\times$	20	6
80		
4		

$=$

10

$\times$	60	3
50		
9		

$=$

Use the grid method.

11 27×74 **13** 95×19

12 68×42 **14** 73×36

C

Copy and complete.

1

$\times$	600	10	5
100			
90			
5			

$=$

2

$\times$	200	40	8
300			
40			
6			

$=$

3

$\times$	300	90	0
400			
70			
1			

$=$

4

$\times$	400	20	7
200			
60			
3			

$=$

Use the grid method.

5 517×228

6 461×284

7 $16\,287 \times 4$

8 1893×46

9 375×369

10 584×436

On this page you will learn a standard method for short multiplication.

Examples

Method 1.

```
                273
          ×       8
200 × 8        1600
 70 × 8         560
  3 × 8          24
               2184
                 1
```

Method 2.

```
          273    Work from the
    ×       8    right and carry.
         2184
          ·5 2
```

A

Work out

1. $(100 × 2) + (40 × 2) + (8 × 2)$
2. $(200 × 3) + (50 × 3) + (6 × 3)$
3. $(200 × 6) + (30 × 6) + (4 × 6)$

4. $(100 × 4) + (70 × 4) + (9 × 4)$
5. $(400 × 9) + (20 × 9) + (3 × 9)$
6. $(500 × 7) + (30 × 7) + (2 × 7)$

Copy and complete.

7.
```
              124
        ×       8
100 × 8
 20 × 8
  4 × 8       ____
```

8.
```
              278
        ×       5
200 × 5
 70 × 5
  8 × 5       ____
```

9.
```
              352
        ×       9
300 × 9
 50 × 9
  2 × 9       ____
```

B

Use Method 1.

```
1      176      5      239
     ×   5           ×   8

2      258      6      386
     ×   7           ×   4

3      249      7      658
     ×   6           ×   7

4      346      8      549
     ×            ×   3
```

Use Method 2.

```
9      167     13      456
     ×   3           ×   8

10     257     14      348
     ×   6           ×   7

11     135     15      829
     ×   9           ×   5

12     329     16      289
     ×   7           ×   8
```

C

Use Method 2.

```
1      486
     ×   3

2      573
     ×   6

3     1847
     ×   8

4     2792
     ×   7

5     5483
     ×   4

6     2875
     ×   9
```

Use Method 2.

7. $3936 × 7$
8. $2648 × 9$
9. $3759 × 8$
10. $5273 × 4$
11. $4349 × 6$
12. $1963 × 9$

On this page you will learn a standard method for long multiplication.

Examples

$$
\begin{array}{r}
46 \\
\times\ 13 \\
\hline
460 \\
138 \\
\hline
598 \\
\end{array}
$$

46 × 10   460
46 × 3   138

$$
\begin{array}{r}
46 \\
\times\ 35 \\
\hline
1380 \\
230 \\
\hline
1610 \\
\end{array}
$$

46 × 30   1380
46 × 5   230

Check by approximating.
40 × 30 = 1200
50 × 40 = 2000
46 × 35 lies between 1200 and 2000.

A

Work out
1. (26 × 10) + (26 × 3)
2. (29 × 10) + (29 × 2)
3. (24 × 10) + (24 × 4)
4. (28 × 10) + (28 × 5)

Copy and complete.

5.
$$
\begin{array}{r}
27 \\
\times\ 14 \\
\end{array}
$$
27 × 10
27 × 4   ___

6.
$$
\begin{array}{r}
35 \\
\times\ 18 \\
\end{array}
$$
35 × 10
35 × 8   ___

7.
$$
\begin{array}{r}
29 \\
\times\ 13 \\
\end{array}
$$
29 × 10
29 × 3   ___

8.
$$
\begin{array}{r}
46 \\
\times\ 15 \\
\end{array}
$$
46 × 10
46 × 5   ___

B

Copy and complete.

1.
$$
\begin{array}{r}
68 \\
\times\ 34 \\
\end{array}
$$
68 × 30
68 × 4   ___

2.
$$
\begin{array}{r}
73 \\
\times\ 18 \\
\end{array}
$$
73 × 10
73 × 8   ___

3.
$$
\begin{array}{r}
92 \\
\times\ 27 \\
\end{array}
$$
92 × 20
92 × 7   ___

4.
$$
\begin{array}{r}
65 \\
\times\ 46 \\
\end{array}
$$
65 × 40
65 × 6   ___

5.
$$
\begin{array}{r}
78 \\
\times\ 52 \\
\end{array}
$$

6.
$$
\begin{array}{r}
48 \\
\times\ 37 \\
\end{array}
$$

7.
$$
\begin{array}{r}
39 \\
\times\ 16 \\
\end{array}
$$

8.
$$
\begin{array}{r}
75 \\
\times\ 29 \\
\end{array}
$$

9.
$$
\begin{array}{r}
59 \\
\times\ 34 \\
\end{array}
$$

10.
$$
\begin{array}{r}
68 \\
\times\ 25 \\
\end{array}
$$

C

Copy and complete.

1.
$$
\begin{array}{r}
128 \\
\times\ 19 \\
\end{array}
$$
128 × 10
128 × 9   ___

2.
$$
\begin{array}{r}
247 \\
\times\ 46 \\
\end{array}
$$
247 × 40
247 × 6   ___

3. 171 × 36
4. 365 × 38
5. 247 × 19
6. 192 × 45
7. 464 × 18
8. 259 × 42
9. 373 × 29
10. 416 × 57

11. A party of 237 football supporters travel to an away game by train. Each ticket costs £48. What is the total cost of the tickets?

12. Angie earns £197 each week. How much does she earn in a year?

13. Each can weighs 364 g. What is the weight of 36 cans in kilograms?

On this page you will learn a standard method for the multiplication of decimals.

Examples

4.3×6

$4.0 \times 6 = 24.0$
$0.3 \times 6 = \underline{1.8}$
25.8

2.57×4

$2.0 \times 4 = 8.0$
$0.5 \times 4 = 2.0$
$0.07 \times 4 = \underline{0.28}$
10.28

Check by adding.

2.57
2.57
2.57
$+ \; \underline{2.57}$
$\underline{10.28}$
${\scriptstyle 2\;2}$

Make sure that the decimal points are all in line.

A

Copy and complete.

1 4.3×2 $4.0 \times 2 = \square$
$0.3 \times 2 = \square$
$4.3 \times 2 = \square$

2 5.2×3 $5.0 \times 2 = \square$
$0.2 \times 3 = \square$
$5.2 \times 3 = \square$

3 6.9×4 $6.0 \times 4 = \square$
$0.9 \times 4 = \square$
$6.9 \times 4 = \square$

4 4.8×5 $4.0 \times 5 = \square$
$0.8 \times 5 = \square$
$4.8 \times 5 = \square$

5 9.7×3 $9.0 \times 3 = \square$
$0.7 \times 3 = \square$
$9.7 \times 3 = \square$

6 7.6×3 $7.0 \times 3 = \square$
$0.2 \times 3 = \square$
$7.2 \times 3 = \square$

B

Work out

1 7.9×3 **7** 6.7×4
2 4.3×6 **8** 7.8×5
3 9.8×2 **9** 3.4×9
4 8.2×7 **10** 5.8×3
5 2.7×9 **11** 9.6×5
6 4.3×8 **12** 3.5×7

13 One mile is about 1.6 kilometres. How far is 4 miles in kilometres?

14 A bucket holds 8.7 litres of water. How much water would 6 buckets hold?

15 A baby weighs 6.4 kilograms. His mother is nine times heavier. How much does his mother weigh?

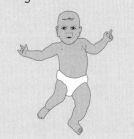

C

Work out

1 3.87×2 **7** 7.34×6
2 2.36×5 **8** 0.96×4
3 4.52×3 **9** 6.45×8
4 5.14×9 **10** 3.06×9
5 0.28×7 **11** 4.28×9
6 5.43×7 **12** 2.78×5

13 A roll of wallpaper is 3.16 metres in length. How long are 8 rolls altogether?

14 A leaking pipe loses 8.75 litres of water in one day. How much water is lost in a week?

15 One gallon is 4.55 litres. How much is three gallons in litres?

16 A cross-country circuit is 1.78 km long. The athletes run the circuit five times. How far do they run altogether?

On this page you will learn an informal method for division.

Examples

$231 \div 6$

Approximate $180 \div 6 = 30$

$\qquad\qquad 240 \div 6 = 40$

$\qquad\qquad 231 \div 6$ lies between 30 and 40

Calculate
```
      231
  −    60    (10 × 6)
      171
  −   120    (20 × 6)
       51
  −    48    (8 × 6)
        3
```

Answer 38 remainder 3

$678 \div 24$

$678 \div 24$ is approximately $700 \div 25 = 28$

```
      678
  −   240    (10 × 24)
      438
  −   240    (10 × 24)
      198
  −   120    (5 × 24)
       78
  −    72    (3 × 24)
        6
```

Answer 28 remainder 6

A

Work out

1. $36 \div 2$
2. $85 \div 5$
3. $74 \div 6$
4. $140 \div 8$
9. $120 \div 9$
10. $134 \div 6$
11. $98 \div 6$
12. $75 \div 4$

5. $93 \div 4$
6. $100 \div 7$
7. $53 \div 3$
8. $61 \div 4$
13. $69 \div 5$
14. $121 \div 7$
15. $200 \div 9$
16. $49 \div 3$

17. In one week a vet treated 112 animals. One quarter were dogs. How many were not dogs?

B

Work out

1. $86 \div 4$
2. $93 \div 6$
3. $159 \div 7$
4. $173 \div 8$
9. $301 \div 8$
10. $294 \div 9$
11. $173 \div 4$
12. $211 \div 6$

5. $129 \div 9$
6. $114 \div 4$
7. $167 \div 6$
8. $205 \div 7$
13. $293 \div 7$
14. $254 \div 8$
15. $350 \div 9$
16. $267 \div 4$

17. Chairs are stacked in groups of 6. How many stacks are needed to store 138 chairs?

18. There are eight screws in each packet. How many packets can be filled with 208 screws?

C

1. $380 \div 15$
2. $514 \div 23$
3. $678 \div 32$
4. $522 \div 16$
5. $551 \div 29$
6. $663 \div 26$
7. $406 \div 19$
8. $879 \div 24$
9. $921 \div 34$
10. $648 \div 18$
11. $608 \div 37$
12. $553 \div 21$

13. The 14 sweets in a packet weigh 322 g. What is the weight of each sweet?

14. Saheed saves the same amount of money each week. After 24 weeks he has saved £816. How much does he save each week?

15. One in every fifteen raffle tickets wins a prize. 435 tickets are sold. How many prizes are needed?

On this page you will learn a standard written method for division.

Examples

METHOD 1

$196 \div 6$

```
  6 ) 196
 −    180    (30 × 6)
      16
 −    12     (2 × 6)
      4
```

Answer 32 R4

METHOD 2

$196 \div 6$

```
       32 R4
  6 ) 196
 −    18     (3 × 6)
      16
 −    12     (2 × 6)
      4
```

METHOD 3

$884 \div 26$

```
       34
 26 ) 884
 −   780     (30 × 26)
     104
 −   104     (4 × 26)
       0
```

A

Use Method 1.

1. $48 \div 2$
2. $112 \div 7$
3. $85 \div 5$
4. $102 \div 6$
5. $78 \div 3$
6. $152 \div 8$
7. $128 \div 4$
8. $126 \div 9$
9. $170 \div 5$
10. $84 \div 6$
11. $147 \div 3$
12. $112 \div 8$
13. $176 \div 4$
14. $198 \div 9$
15. $133 \div 7$
16. $136 \div 8$

17. There are eight cakes in each box. How many boxes can be filled from 112 cakes?

18. Six train tickets cost £96. How much does one ticket cost?

19. Kym has read one third of her book. The book has 228 pages. How many pages has she read?

20. Four friends share a prize of £268. How much should each person receive?

B

Use Method 2.

1. $138 \div 6$
2. $314 \div 7$
3. $250 \div 8$
4. $423 \div 9$
5. $347 \div 6$
6. $183 \div 7$
7. $224 \div 8$
8. $687 \div 9$
9. $201 \div 6$
10. $369 \div 7$
11. $377 \div 8$
12. $348 \div 9$
13. $290 \div 6$
14. $272 \div 7$
15. $530 \div 8$
16. $833 \div 9$

17. There were 245 passengers on a plane. One seventh of the passengers got off at Paris. How many flew on to New York?

18. Eight magazines weigh 536 grams. How much does one weigh?

C

Use Method 3.

1. $13 \overline{)351}$
2. $15 \overline{)405}$
3. $14 \overline{)322}$
4. $19 \overline{)646}$
5. $17 \overline{)731}$
6. $22 \overline{)770}$
7. $26 \overline{)390}$
8. $25 \overline{)925}$
9. $24 \overline{)696}$
10. $27 \overline{)432}$

11. A school needs 450 exercise books. They are sold in packs of 24. How many packs will the school need to order? How many books will be left over?

12. The 728 children in a school are divided equally into 28 classes. How many children are there in each class?

On this page you will learn:

• to recognise a negative number output.

Example   5 − 8

Press | C | 5 | − | 8 | = | ⟶   −3

• to key in and interpret money calculations.

Example   £3·12 × 5

Press | C | 3 | · | 1 | 2 | × | 5 | = | ⟶   15·6.   Answer = £15·60

• to carry out calculations involving more than one step.

Example   7 × (315 ÷ 9)   Key in operation in brackets first.

Press | C | 3 | 1 | 5 | ÷ | 9 | × | 7 | = | ⟶   245

A

Use a calculator to work out the problems and interpret the display.

1 6 − 11	**6** 5 − 26	**11** £8·30 − 65p	**16** £9·17 − £2·77
2 9 − 17	**7** 1 − 30	**12** £6·07 − 49p	**17** 89 + (19 × 7)
3 4 − 19	**8** 10 − 32	**13** £2·52 + 3·78	**18** 9 × (93 − 46)
4 7 − 23	**9** £2·60 + 84p	**14** £12·64 − £1·94	**19** 5 × (282 ÷ 6)
5 3 − 16	**10** £3·90 + 67p	**15** £4·63 + £2·87	**20** 4 × (333 ÷ 9)

B

1 26 − 41	**6** 27 − 64	**11** £6·00 − 75p − 38p	**16** £31·20 ÷ 12
2 31 − 48	**7** 17 − 93	**12** £9·00 − 59p − 64p	**17** 3·12 + (6·72 × 4)
3 19 − 75	**8** 43 − 78	**13** £2·24 × 15	**18** 15·67 + (9·37 × 9)
4 14 − 57	**9** £3·20 + 64p	**14** £4·35 × 8	**19** 5 × (2·46 + 1·34)
5 35 − 86	**10** £4·90 + 85p	**15** £50·40 ÷ 14	**20** 6 × (12·1 − 5·6)

C

1 1·2 − 6·7	**6** 4·71 − 9·3	**11** 8·96 + (4·56 × 9)	**16** (£2·57 + 78p) × 8
2 4·5 − 8·65	**7** 1·2 − 7·43	**12** 8 × (16·2 − 12·7)	**17** 6 × (£6·24 − 89p)
3 3·2 − 5·91	**8** 5·81 − 12·47	**13** (£21·92 + 88p) ÷ 6	**18** (£29·63 + 77p) ÷ 8
4 7·9 − 11·36	**9** 3·48 + (2·6 × 7)	**14** (£18·83 + 77p) ÷ 5	**19** (£23·45 − 59p) ÷ 9
5 2·3 − 4·86	**10** 5 × (9·2 − 3·8)	**15** 5 × (£3·45 − 69p)	**20** (£4·13 × 4) ÷ 7

On this page you will use a calculator to solve problems.

A

Copy and complete.

1. $86 + \square = 175$
2. $\square + 59 = 243$
3. $165 + \square = 218$
4. $\square + 67 = 123$
5. $135 - \square = 57$
6. $\square - 86 = 161$
7. $253 - \square = 175$
8. $\square - 127 = 248$
9. $318 - \square = 149$
10. $\square + 137 = 283$
11. $712 - \square = 464$
12. $\square - 254 = 379$

13. Find pairs of consecutive numbers which add up to:
    a) 65 c) 211
    b) 143 d) 275.

14. The temperature is 14°C. It falls 36°C. What is the new temperature?

15. Zoe saves £2·40 each week. How much has she saved after 14 weeks?

16. 29,448 people live in Bashley. One twelfth of the population of the town is over 75. How many people are over 75 in Bashley?

B

Copy and complete.

1. $1·37 + \square = 2·6$
2. $2·58 + \square = 4·19$
3. $\square + 0·86 = 4·35$
4. $\square + 1·64 = 3·28$
5. $3·45 - \square = 1·7$
6. $5·28 - \square = 3·61$
7. $\square - 1·63 = 0·79$
8. $\square - 2·37 = 1·85$

9. Find three consecutive numbers which add up to:
   a) 81   c) 195
   b) 114   d) 222.

10. Find three sevenths of 3598.

11. A school buys a set of books for £178·20. Each book costs £4·95. How many books does the school buy?

12. At the Equator the temperature is 34°C. At the North Pole it is 87°C colder. What is the temperature at the North Pole?

C

1. A supermarket needs 10 000 apples. A crate holds 48 apples. How many crates does the supermarket need to order?

2. Tickets for a charity concert cost £4·50. 629 people attend the concert. How much money is raised by the sale of tickets?

3. A lake is 127 metres deep. The surface of the lake is 73 metres above sea level. How many metres below sea level is the bottom of the lake?

4. A burger bar sells 276 burgers. The takings for the burgers is £372·60. How much does each burger cost?

5. Two ninths of the 39 357 spectators at a football match are children. How many adults are at the match?

6. Which number, when multiplied by itself, gives a product of:
   a) 256   c) 529
   b) 361   d) 1369?

On this page you will learn to recognise the operation in a number sentence.

Examples

$238 \square 127 = 365$ The missing sign is $+$. $30 \square 12.5 = 17.5$ The missing sign is $-$.

$17 \square 6 = 102$ The missing sign is $\times$. $42 \square 4 = 10.5$ The missing sign is $\div$.

A

Copy and complete.

1 $30 \square 8 = 240$

2 $80 \square 35 = 45$

3 $87 \square 36 = 123$

4 $60 \square 4 = 15$

5 $68 \square 39 = 29$

6 $135 \square 90 = 225$

7 $12 \square 6 = 72$

8 $69 \square 3 = 23$

B

Copy and complete.

1 $19 \square 7 = 133$

2 $316 \square 174 = 490$

3 $3.7 \square 2.4 = 1.3$

4 $523 \square 88 = 435$

5 $46 \square 18 = 828$

6 $486 \square 9 = 54$

7 $120 \square 24 = 5$

8 $8.3 \square 1.6 = 9.9$

C

Copy and complete.

1 $646 \square 34 = 19$

2 $7.28 \square 3.19 = 4.09$

3 $1926 \square 1437 = 3363$

4 $456 \square 19 = 8664$

5 $54.2 \square 7 = 379.4$

6 $1000 \square 64.8 = 935.2$

7 $32.7 \square 84.54 = 117.24$

8 $328 \square 8 = 41$

 Now you will learn to make up stories to match number sentences.

Examples

$35 \times 28 = 980$
A theatre has 35 rows of 28 seats.
The theatre has 980 seats.

$29 \div 4 = 7.25$
29 m of cloth is cut into four equal lengths.
Each length is 7.25 m.

A

Make up a story to match each number sentence.

1 $48 + 37 = 85$

2 $97 - 42 = 55$

3 $19 \times 4 = 76$

4 $450 \div 3 = 150$

5 $326 + 64 = 390$

6 $200 - 120 = 80$

7 $60 \times 5 = 300$

8 $58 \div 2 = 29$

B

Make up a story to match each number sentence.

1 $3.4 + 1.7 = 5.1$

2 $6 - 4.2 = 1.8$

3 $248 \times 7 = 1736$

4 $232 \div 8 = 29$

5 $463 + 179 = 642$

6 $435 - 78 = 357$

7 $16.5 \times 26 = 429$

8 $28.8 \div 9 = 3.2$

C

Make up a story to match each number sentence.

1 $159.6 + 63.75 = 223.35$

2 $42.9 - 28.65 = 14.25$

3 $5.36 \times 24 = 128.64$

4 $49.6 \div 8 = 6.2$

5 $0.05 + 0.03 = 0.08$

6 $19.2 - 3.64 = 15.56$

7 $27 \times 36 = 972$

8 $144 \div 40 = 3.6$

On this page you will learn to find examples that match a general statement.

Example

Dividing a number by 10 moves every digit one place to the right.

$1\,340 \div 10 = 134$ $2\,178 \div 10 = 217{\cdot}8$

Find two examples that match these statements.

1. A multiple of 4 is also a multiple of 2.

2. A multiple of 10 is always twice a multiple of 5.

3. A number is not a multiple of 5 if it does not end in a 5 or a 0.

4. The square of any even number is even.

5. If you add two different numbers the other way round the answer is the same.

6. Multiplying a number by 10 moves every digit one place to the left.

B

Find three examples that match these statements.

1. A multiple of 6 is also a multiple of 3.

2. A multiple of 8 is always twice a multiple of 4.

3. A number is a multiple of 4 if its last two digits are divisible by 4.

4. The product of any two consecutive numbers is even.

5. If you multiply different numbers the other way round the answer is the same.

6. Multiplying a number by 100 moves every digit two places to the left.

7. The angles on a straight line add up to $180°$.

C

Find four examples that match these statements.

1. A multiple of 8 is also a multiple of 2.

2. A multiple of 9 is always three times a multiple of 3.

3. A number is a multiple of 3 if the sum of its digits is divisible by 3.

4. The square of any odd number is odd.

5. If you divide different numbers the other way round the answer is different.

6. Dividing a number by 100 moves every digit two places to the right.

7. The angles at a point add up to $360°$.

On these pages you will learn:

- to choose the operation or operations needed to solve word problems.

- to decide whether the calculation will be done mentally or on paper.

- to use all four operations to solve the problems.

Some of the problems require one operation only. Some require more than one.

David has 78 photos.
Lindsey has 36.
How many do they
have altogether?

$78 + 36 = 114$

They have 114 photos altogether.

David has 66 books.
Lindsey has 35 more.
How many do they
have altogether?

$66 + 35 = 101$
$101 + 66 = 167$

They have 167 books altogether.

In each section read the problems and decide:

a) what operations are needed.

b) whether the calculation will be done mentally or on paper.

Then solve the problems.

A

1 Two thirds of the 27 passengers on a bus are adults. How many of the passengers are children?

2 There are 12 biscuits in each packet. How many biscuits are there in 6 packets?

3 Mark is 18. His father is 38 years older. How old is Mark's father?

4 There are 74 apples on a tree. 19 are picked. How many apples are there on the tree now?

5 Rachel has four CD towers. Each tower has 35 CDs. How many CDs does Rachel have?

6 Komal has read one fifth of her book. She has just read page 24. How many pages does the book have?

7 There are 42 cars in a car park. In the next hour 29 enter and 53 leave. How many cars are there now in the car park?

8 The 60 children in Year 5 were asked what pets they owned. One quarter of the children had no pets at all, 12 had cats and 17 had dogs. How many children had other sorts of pets?

9 A video shop had three racks with 80 videos and four racks with 120 videos. How many videos are there on the racks?

10 All of Mrs. Carter's seven children had four children themselves. All of her grandchildren had three children each. How many great grandchildren does Mrs. Carter have?

B

1. This year there will be 190 school days. How many days will not be school days?

2. A car travels 9 miles per litre of petrol. How many litres of petrol will be used in travelling 108 miles?

3. Paul has read 45 pages of his book. He needs to read 26 more to reach half way. How many pages does Paul's book have?

4. There are 80 tea bags in a box. How many boxes will 400 tea bags fill?

5. 134 parents watched the afternoon performance of the School Concert. 97 more came that evening. How many parents saw the evening performance?

6. There are 116 passengers on a train. At the next station 48 people get off and 57 get on. How many passengers are there now?

7. Sharon has 200 chocolate drops. On Monday she eats one fifth of the sweets. On Tuesday she eats one half of the rest. How many chocolate drops are left?

8. 303 children in a school go on a trip. Five coaches each carry 51 children. The rest travel by minibus, each of which can carry 13 children. How many minibuses are there?

9. How many minutes are there in a day?

10. Max has 175 photos. He keeps 79 photos in one album. The rest are equally divided between three more identical albums. How many photos are there in each of Max's identical albums?

C

1. There are 24 Jaffa cakes in each box. How many boxes are needed for 1200 cakes?

2. Bradley swims 50 lengths of a pool every day. How many lengths would he swim in April?

3. 62 386 people watched Manchester United's match on Wednesday. How many saw the next match when there were 649 fewer spectators?

4. There are 260 people watching a film. Two fifths of the audience are adults. How many children are watching the film?

5. During the day 257 books are returned to a library and 149 are borrowed. At the end of the day there are 2 415 books. How many books were there in the library at the start of the day?

6. There are 342 passengers on a flight leaving London. At New York 153 people get off the plane and 79 new passengers get on. How many people are on the plane when it flies on to Los Angeles?

7. There are 4 wards on every floor of a hospital. Each ward has 20 beds. How many floors are there if the hospital has 560 beds altogether?

8. How many seconds are there in five hours?

9. The garden centre had eight trays with 24 potted plants in each. Another six trays had 30 plants in each. 143 plants were sold. How many plants were left?

10. There are 120 sugar cubes in a packet. How many packets could 3 000 sugar cubes fill?

On this page you will solve problems involving money using all four operations.

SUPER SPORTS - PRICE LIST

Leather footballs £16·50	Tennis balls 4 for £3·00	Ping pong balls 6 for £1·50
Shuttlecocks 10 for £2·20		Plastic footballs £3·75
Tennis rackets £17·55	Badminton rackets £11·25	Table tennis bats £6·70
Football boots £23·00		Trainers £23·40
Football shirt £19·80	Goalkeeper's gloves £3·15	Snooker table £85·00

A

Use the price list to work out the cost of the purchase and the change from £50.

1 a football shirt and a pair of trainers

2 4 table tennis bats and 6 ping pong balls

3 2 leather footballs and a pair of goalkeeper's gloves

4 10 plastic footballs

5 2 tennis rackets and 4 tennis balls

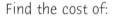

Find the cost of:

6 1 tennis ball

7 1 shuttlecock

8 1 ping pong ball

9 20 tennis balls

10 5 shuttlecocks

11 36 ping pong balls.

12 How many badminton rackets could you buy for £100?

13 How many leather footballs could you buy for £100?

14 You buy a tennis racket and one other item for £24·25. What is that item?

15 You buy a pair of trainers and one other item for £43·20. What is that item?

16 Gareth saves up his 50 pence coins.
How many 50ps will he need to save before he can buy a snooker table?

17 Gillian saves up her 20 pence coins.
How many will she need to save before she can buy a pair of trainers?

B

Use the price list. Work out the cost of each purchase and the change from £100.

1. 4 badminton rackets and 20 shuttlecocks
2. 5 football shirts
3. 3 pairs of trainers and a pair of football boots
4. 12 table tennis bats and 30 ping pong balls
5. 8 pairs of goalkeeper's gloves

Find the cost of:

6. 3 tennis balls
7. 7 shuttlecocks
8. 5 ping pong balls
9. 100 shuttlecocks
10. 10 football shirts
11. 20 plastic footballs.

12. Copy and complete the table by changing the pounds to the foreign currencies.

U.K. (pound)	S. Africa (rand)	U.S.A. (dollar)	Japan (yen)
£1·00	10	1·6	170
£10·00			
£50·00			
£300·00			

C

Use the price list. Work out the cost of each purchase and the change from £500.

1. 21 pairs of trainers
2. 20 leather footballs and 6 pairs of football boots
3. 24 football shirts
4. 8 badminton rackets and 50 shuttlecocks
5. 12 tennis rackets and 60 tennis balls

6. How many plastic footballs could a school buy for £100?
7. How many badminton rackets could be bought for £150?
8. A youth club buys 8 table tennis bats and one other item for £70·10. What is that item?

9. Copy and complete the table by changing the pounds to the foreign currencies.

U.K. (pound)	India (rupee)	Europe (Euro)	Israel (shekel)
£1·00	69	1·64	6·15
£10·00			
£80·00			
£200·00			

On these pages you will learn:

- **to use the relationship between metric units of length.**

$$10\,mm = 1\,cm$$
$$5\,mm = 0{\cdot}5\,cm$$
$$1\,mm = 0{\cdot}1\,cm$$

$$100\,cm = 1\,m$$
$$50\,cm = 0{\cdot}5\,m$$
$$10\,cm = 0{\cdot}1\,m$$
$$1\,cm = 0{\cdot}01\,m$$

$$1000\,m = 1\,km$$
$$500\,m = 0{\cdot}5\,km$$
$$100\,m = 0{\cdot}1\,km$$
$$10\,m = 0{\cdot}01\,km$$
$$1\,m = 0{\cdot}001\,km$$

Examples

7 mm = ☐ cm   Answer   0·7 cm

☐ cm = 0·8 m   Answer   80 cm

214 m = ☐ km   Answer   0·214 km

- **to suggest suitable units to measure lengths.**

If the length is less than 1 cm use millimetres.

If the length is less than 1 m use centimetres.

If the length is less than 1 km use metres.

A

Copy and complete by writing the missing number in the box.

1. 0·5 km = ☐ m
2. 0·6 km = ☐ m
3. 1100 m = ☐ km
4. 3700 m = ☐ km
5. 1·5 m = ☐ cm
6. 0·8 m = ☐ cm
7. 250 cm = ☐ m
8. 140 cm = ☐ m
9. 0·3 cm = ☐ mm
10. 2·7 cm = ☐ mm
11. 15 mm = ☐ cm
12. 31 mm = ☐ cm

Suggest a suitable metric unit to measure these lengths.

13. a lollipop stick
14. a ladybird
15. the height of a block of flats
16. a pea
17. the Channel tunnel
18. a straw

Think of three more things you would measure using:

19. centimetres
20. metres
21. kilometres.

Write the longest length from each pair.

22. 25 m   0·25 km
23. 33 mm   3 cm
24. 8 cm   0·8 m
25. 14·6 cm   46 mm
26. 600 m   6 km
27. 55 cm   0·5 m

B

Copy and complete.

1 2·7 km = ☐ m

2 1·38 km = ☐ m

3 3600 m = ☐ km

4 2570 m = ☐ km

5 1·4 m = ☐ cm

6 3·61 m = ☐ cm

7 528 cm = ☐ m

8 217 cm = ☐ m

9 2·9 cm = ☐ mm

10 1·5 cm = ☐ mm

11 3 mm = ☐ cm

12 98 mm = ☐ cm

Suggest a suitable metric unit to measure these lengths.

13 a staple

14 the length of the River Nile

15 a school corridor

16 an ear stud

17 a fork

18 a plane journey

Think of three more things you would measure using:

19 millimetres **21** metres

20 centimetres **22** kilometres.

Copy and complete by putting >, < or = in the box.

23 4·9 cm ☐ 490 mm

24 720 mm ☐ 0·72 m

25 100 m ☐ 0·08 km

26 250 m ☐ 0·25 km

27 9·9 cm ☐ 0·1 m

28 66 cm ☐ 0·166 m

C

Copy and complete the tables.

1

mm	m
1 →	0·001
2480 →	
→	0·007
→	0·150

3

m	km
287 →	0·287
3281 →	
→	1·594
→	2·3

2

cm	m
6 →	0·06
159 →	
→	1·3
→	0·47

4

mm	cm
30 →	3
4 →	
→	1·7
→	0·1

Copy and complete by choosing the best estimate.

5 The length of a pen is (140 mm, 140 cm, 140 m).

6 The competitors in a marathon run (420 m, 4200 m, 42 000 m).

7 The width of a computer screen is (0·3 m, 0·03 m, 0·003 m).

8 The distance from London to Brighton is (800 m, 80 000 m, 800 km).

9 The length of an oval running track is (4 km, 0·4 km, 40 km).

10 The diameter of a CD is (12 mm, 1·2 cm, 0·12 m).

Arrange these lengths in ascending order.

11 44 cm   0·4 m   404 mm   0·004 km

12 0·338 km   38 m   380 cm   0·38 km

13 55 mm   0·05 m   0·5 m   5·5 mm

14 27 m   0·02 km   0·007 km   2007 cm

15 109 m   9000 mm   0·19 km   109 cm

On this page you will learn to solve problems involving length.

A

1. One shelf is 65 cm long. Another shelf is 78 cm long. What is their total length in metres?

2. Lisa is 1·50 m tall. Shaun is 35 cm shorter. How tall is Shaun in metres?

3. Gary needs 10 pieces of ribbon. Each piece must be 50 cm long. How many metres of ribbon does he need to buy?

4. A machine makes a staple from 20 mm of wire. How many staples will it make from 50 cm of wire?

5. Grace walks 80 m in one minute. How far does she walk in one hour in kilometres?

6. Ethan's middle finger is 10·6 cm long. His ring finger is 9 mm shorter. How long is his ring finger in centimetres?

B

1. A cyclist travels 2 km in eight minutes. How far in metres does she cycle in one minute?

2. Jacob jumps 1·95 m. The winning jump is 17 cm higher. What is the height of the winning jump?

3. A golf hole is 0·43 km long. A golfer drives the ball 264 m. How much further does he have to play?

4. There are 24 tiles in a stack. Each tile is 8 mm thick. How high is the stack in centimetres?

5. Each paper tissue is 20 cm long. How many metres of paper are needed to fill a box with 150 tissues?

6. Stuart is 1·28 m tall. His father is 38 cm taller. How tall is Stuart's father?

C

1. Samantha saws four strips of 52 cm from a 3 m length of wood. How long is the wood that is left?

2. A table has a perimeter of 5 m. It is 68 cm wide. What is its length?

3. A set of encyclopaedias takes up 96 cm of shelving. Each volume is 32 mm wide. How many encyclopaedias are there in the set?

4. An athlete trains by running 300 m eight times and 200 m six times. How far does he run in kilometres?

5. A mineshaft is 0·78 km long. A further 367 m is drilled. How long is the mineshaft in metres?

6. A candle is 12 cm tall. 36 mm is used. How long is the candle that is left in centimetres?

On this page you will learn to read scales accurately.

For each of the scales work out
a) the measurement indicated by each of the arrows.
b) the difference between the two arrows.

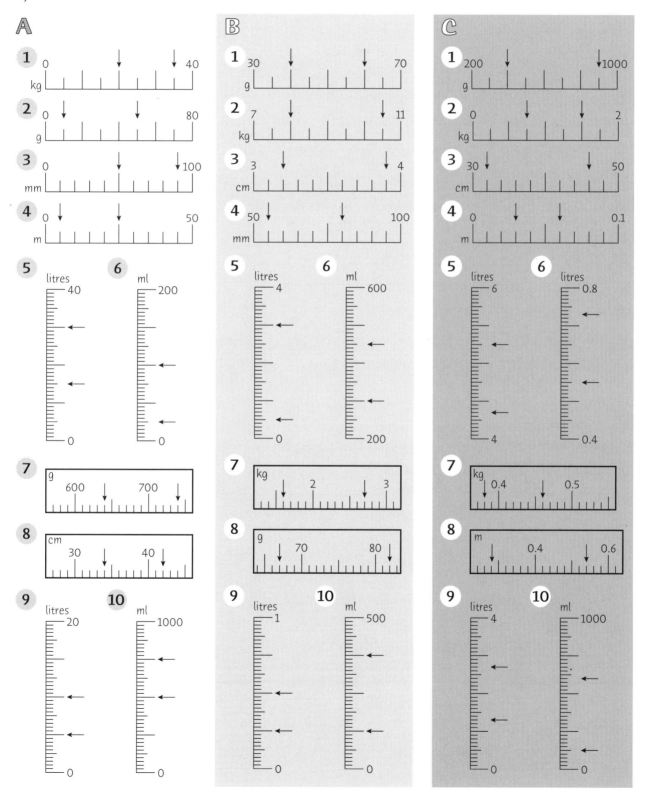

On this page you will learn to use the metric measures of mass, grams and kilograms.

$1000\,g = 1\,kg$ $500\,g = 0{\cdot}500\,kg = 0{\cdot}5\,kg$ $100\,g = 0{\cdot}100\,kg = 0{\cdot}1\,kg$

A

Copy and complete by writing the missing number in the box.

1. $2\,kg = \square\,g$
2. $1{\cdot}500\,kg = \square\,g$
3. $0{\cdot}250\,kg = \square\,g$
4. $1{\cdot}9\,kg = \square\,g$
5. $750\,g = \square\,kg$
6. $5200\,g = \square\,kg$
7. $1250\,g = \square\,kg$
8. $2400\,g = \square\,kg$
9. $3{\cdot}750\,kg = \square\,g$
10. $0{\cdot}8\,kg = \square\,g$
11. $400\,g = \square\,kg$
12. $5500\,g = \square\,kg$

Which metric unit would you use to measure the mass of:

13. a light bulb
14. a wardrobe
15. a spoon
16. a dog?

B

Copy and complete by writing the missing number in the box.

1. $3\,kg = \square\,g$
2. $1{\cdot}750\,kg = \square\,g$
3. $0{\cdot}600\,kg = \square\,g$
4. $2{\cdot}960\,kg = \square\,g$
5. $2480\,g = \square\,kg$
6. $800\,g = \square\,kg$
7. $3500\,g = \square\,kg$
8. $620\,g = \square\,kg$
9. $6{\cdot}25\,kg = \square\,g$
10. $1{\cdot}8\,kg = \square\,g$
11. $4350\,g = \square\,kg$
12. $940\,g = \square\,kg$

Which metric unit would you use to measure the mass of:

13. a set of encyclopaedias
14. an egg
15. a piano
16. a telephone?

C

Copy and complete the tables.

1.

g	kg
1386	→
600	→
5160	→
→	4
→	2·98
→	0·641

2.

kg	g
6·5	→
0·075	→
3·25	→
→	394
→	3700
→	45

Copy and complete each sentence by choosing the best estimate.

3. At birth many babies have a mass of about (0·35 kg, 3·5 kg, 35 kg).

4. One pound coins have a mass of about (1 g, 10 g, 100 g).
5. Many footballers weigh about (70 kg, 700 kg, 7000 kg).
6. A tin of beans has a mass of about (0·004 kg, 0·04 kg, 0·4 kg).

On this page you will solve problems involving mass.

A

1. A tin of fruit weighs 200 g. What do 8 tins weigh in kilograms?

2. Four melons weigh 2 kg. What does one melon weigh?

3. Tom weighs 42·3 kg. Jerry weighs 1800 g less. What is their combined weight?

4. A sack of potatoes weighs 5 kg. Three quarters of the potatoes are eaten. What is the weight of the potatoes that are left?

5. A 200 g pack of ham contains 8 slices. How much does each slice weigh?

6. A cake is cut into 10 slices, each of which weighs 140 g. What is the weight of the cake in kilograms?

B

1. The 20 packets of biscuits in a box weigh 6 kg altogether. What is the weight of one packet in grams?

2. Each apple weighs 150 g. How much do 12 apples weigh in kilogrammes?

3. A piece of cheese weighs 0·5 kg. 230 g of the cheese is eaten. How much is left?

4. A casserole is made with 800 g of meat and 1·2 kg of vegetables. What is the combined weight of the ingredients?

5. 10 packets of gravy powder weigh 3·5 kg. What does one packet weigh?

6. A box of lettuces weighs 2 kg. If the box weighs 100 g, how much do the lettuces weigh?

C

1. A loaf of bread weighs 0·8 kg. It is cut into 25 equal slices. How much does each slice weigh?

2. One parcel weighs 470 g. A second parcel weighs 200 g more. What is the combined weight of the parcels in kilograms?

3. A factory canteen serves 400 lunches. Each lunch requires 300 g of potatoes. What weight of potatoes is used?

4. A recipe for 8 people requires using 1 kg of mince. How much mince would you use if you were cooking for 3 people?

5. A builder needs 2 kg of sand. He has 680 g left. How much more sand does he need?

6. A box containing 16 tins weighs 4 kg. How much does each tin weigh?

On this page you wil learn to use the metric measures of capacity, litres and millilitres.

1000 ml = 1 litre   500 ml = 0·500 litres   250 ml = 0·250 litres   100 ml = 0·100 litres

                 = 0·5 litres   = 0·25 litres   = 0·1 litres

A

Copy and complete by writing the missing number in the box.

1. 1 litre = ☐ ml
2. 1·25 litres = ☐ ml
3. 0·75 litres = ☐ ml
4. 2·300 litres = ☐ ml

5. 3000 ml = ☐ litres
6. 2500 ml = ☐ litres
7. 250 ml = ☐ litres
8. 1900 ml = ☐ litres

9. 3·5 litres = ☐ ml
10. 0·6 litres = ☐ ml
11. 400 ml = ☐ litres
12. 3750 ml = ☐ litres

Which metric unit would you use to measure the capacity of:

13. a washing machine

14. a spoonful of medicine
15. an eyebath
16. a paddling pool
17. a can of cola
18. a stream?

B

Copy and complete by writing the missing number in the box.

1. 5 litres = ☐ ml
2. 2·750 litres = ☐ ml
3. 4·320 litres = ☐ ml
4. 0·370 litres = ☐ ml

5. 2380 ml = ☐ litres
6. 700 ml = ☐ litres
7. 1890 ml = ☐ litres
8. 5900 ml = ☐ litres

9. 6·5 litres = ☐ ml
10. 1·8 litres = ☐ ml
11. 2250 ml = ☐ litres
12. 480 ml = ☐ litres

Which metric unit would you use to measure the capacity of:

13. a hot water tank
14. a sachet of vinegar
15. a water pistol
16. a glass of orange
17. a swamp
18. a teapot?

C

Copy and complete the tables.

1.

ml	litres
2280 →	2·28
1347 →	
510 →	
→	4
→	2·94
→	1·681

2.

litres	ml
0·9 →	900
3·92 →	
2·156 →	
→	4659
→	42
→	780

Copy and complete by choosing the best estimate.

3. A squeezy lemon contains (0·015 l, 0·15 l, 1·5 l).

4. A fish tank contains (100 ml, 1000 ml, 10 000 ml) of water.

5. An ink bottle has a capacity of (0·03 l, 0·3 l, 3 l).

6. The petrol tank of a car has a capacity of (40 l, 400 l, 4000 l).

7. A bottle of salad dressing has a capacity of (2·5 ml, 25 ml, 250 ml).

8. A bath has a capacity of (10 l, 100 l, 1000 l).

On this page you will learn to solve problems involving capacity.

A

1. A bottle of lemonade holds one litre. One quarter of it is drunk. How much lemonade is left in the bottle?

2. An ink cartridge holds 15 ml. It can be filled twenty times from an ink bottle. How much ink is in the bottle?

3. Five children share a 2 litre bottle of cola. How much cola does each child have?

4. 200 ml of water is poured into a bowl. One and a half litres is added. How much water is in the bowl?

5. A shower uses 50 ml of water every second. How much water does it use in one minute?

6. Hannah pours 0·2 litres of water into her steam iron. When she has finished ironing there is 40 ml of water left. How much water has turned to steam?

B

1. One quarter of a 2 litre tub of ice cream is used on Tuesday. 350 ml is used on Wednesday. How much ice cream is left?

2. A water pistol holds 120 ml of water. It is filled up 15 times. How much water is squirted from the pistol in litres?

3. 600 ml of paint is needed to paint one fence panel. How many litres of paint will be needed to paint 14 panels?

4. A motor mower has 800 ml of petrol left. 2·7 litres is added. How much petrol is there now?

5. Nathan uses 40 ml of washing up liquid every day. How long will his one litre bottle last?

6. A cafe makes 20 litres of tea in an urn. How many 250 ml cups can be filled?

C

1. 1·2 litres of water and 400 ml of orange are used to make orange squash. It is poured into eight glasses. How much does each glass hold?

2. Twenty-four 150 ml glasses are filled from four one litre bottles of wine. How much wine is left?

3. A sprinkler uses 60 ml of water every second. How many litres does it use in one minute?

4. A puddle contains 12·4 litres of water. 700 ml evaporates. How much water is left?

5. A bottle of handwash contains 300 ml. How many bottles can be filled from 12 litres?

6. A dripping tap loses 35 ml of water every minute. How many litres does it lose in 10 hours?

7. A chemist makes a medicine by mixing 0·8 litres of one liquid with 675 ml of another liquid. How much medicine is made?

On these pages you will learn how to measure and calculate the area and perimeter of a rectangle and other shapes.

The area of a shape is the amount of surface it covers.
It is measured in squares, usually square metres (m^2) or square centimetres (cm^2).

The perimeter of a shape is the distance around its edges.
It is a length and is measured in units of length such as metres or centimetres.

To understand the difference between area and perimeter think of a field.
The perimeter is the fence. The area is the field itself.

Example

Area = length × breadth ($l \times b$)
      = (6×4) cm^2 = 24 cm^2

Perimeter = $2 \times (l + b)$
             = $2 \times (6 + 4)$ cm = 2×10 cm = 20 cm

Measure each shape and work out the perimeter.

1   **2**   **3**

 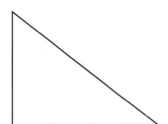 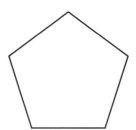

4   Work out the perimeters of these shapes.

    a)   square sides – 7 cm   c)   equilateral triangle – sides 6 cm
    b)   rectangle sides – 8 cm 4 cm   d)   regular pentagon – sides 4 cm

Use 1 cm squared paper. Draw these shapes and work out each area by counting squares.

5   square – 6 cm sides   **7**   square – 4 cm sides

6   rectangle – sides 5 cm 7 cm   **8**   rectangle – sides 4 cm 9 cm

9   Use squared paper. Draw a square with an area of 25 cm^2. Work out the perimeter.

10   Draw a rectangle with a length of 8 cm and a perimeter of 22 cm. Work out the area.

B

Work out the perimeters of these shapes.

1 rectangle – sides 5 cm 12 cm

3 square – sides 4·5 cm

2 regular hexagon – sides 7 cm

4 regular octagon – sides 9 cm

5 Copy and complete this table showing the measurements of rectangles.

Length	5 cm	7 cm		7 cm	8 cm	
Breadth	4 cm	3 cm	5 cm			4 cm
Perimeter			26 cm	28 cm		
Area					24 cm^2	36 cm^2

6 Use squared paper. Draw three different rectangles each with an area of 30 cm^2. Work out the perimeters.

7 Use squared paper. Draw three different rectangles each with a perimeter of 30 cm. Work out the areas.

8 A square playground has a perimeter of 200 metres. What is its area?

C

The lengths of these shapes are in cm. For each shape work out:
a) the perimeter   b) the area.

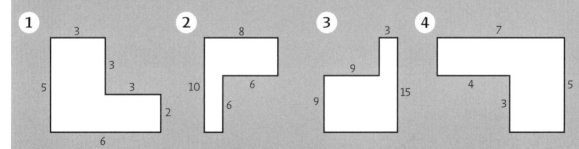

1 3, 3, 5, 3, 2, 6

2 8, 10, 6, 6

3 3, 9, 9, 15

4 7, 4, 3, 5

5 Copy and complete the table showing the measurements of rectangles.

Length	12 cm			3·5 cm		
Breadth		8 cm		4 cm	2·5 cm	
Perimeter	46 cm		30 cm			28 cm
Area		104 cm^2	54 cm^2		15 cm^2	48 cm^2

6 How many square centimetres are there in a square metre?

7 How many square millimetres are there in a square centimetre?

8 How many square metres are there in a square kilometre?

9 A carpet costs £20 per square metre. A room is 6 metres long and 4 metres wide. How much would it cost to carpet the room?

On this page you will learn to use the vocabulary related to time.

You should know and be able to use these facts and this rhyme.

1 millennium	= 1000 years	
1 century	= 100 years	
1 year	= 12 months	
	= 52 weeks	
1 week	= 7 days	
1 day	= 24 hours	
1 hour	= 60 minutes	
1 minute	= 60 seconds	

30 days has September,
April, June and November.
All the rest have 31,
Save for February alone,
Which has but 28 days clear
And 29 in each leap year.

A

Write as minutes.

1 7 hours

2 $4\frac{1}{4}$ hours

3 300 seconds

4 150 seconds

Write as days.

5 3 weeks

6 8 weeks

7 12 hours

8 72 hours

Write as years.

9 4 decades

10 3 centuries

11 24 months

12 6 months

13 How many days are there in:
   a) March
   b) June
   c) May
   d) September
   e) July and August
   f) November and December?

14 Look at the calendar.
   Is this a leap year? How do you know?

15 On what day will these children have their birthday?
   a) Gavin – 4th February
   b) Kate – 23rd February
   c) Davina – 6th March
   d) Amanda – 31st January

FEBRUARY						
Su	M	Tu	W	Th	F	Sa
	1	2	3	4	5	6
7	8	9	10	11	12	13
14	15	16	17	18	19	20
21	22	23	24	25	26	27
28						

16 Christmas Day is a Tuesday.
   What day of the week is New Year's Eve?

17 A school begins its half term holiday on Friday 23rd October. The holiday last one week.
   What is the date of the first Monday back at school?

18 It is June 15th. Levi's birthday is in three weeks time.
   What is the date of his birthday?

B

Write as minutes.

1 8 hours

2 $5\frac{3}{4}$ hours

3 420 seconds

4 210 seconds

Write as weeks.

5 3 years

6 24 months

7 63 days

8 $\frac{1}{2}$ century

Write as years.

9 48 months

10 26 weeks

11 23 decades

12 $\frac{1}{4}$ millennium

13 What will be the date two weeks after:

a) 22nd April   b) 18th September   c) 25th December   d) 19th October?

Look at the calendar for March.

14 On what day of the week do these birthdays fall?

a) Rose – March 13th

b) Meera – March 23rd

c) Marcus – February 25th

d) Sidney – April 12th.

15 Write out the calendar for April 2005.

MARCH 2005						
Su	M	Tu	W	Th	F	Sa
		1	2	3	4	5
6	7	8	9	10	11	12
13	14	15	16	17	18	19
20	21	22	23	24	25	26
27	28	29	30	31		

C

Write True or False for each of the following statements.

1 Five thousand weeks is less than a century.

2 One hour is longer than 3000 seconds.

3 There are less than 1000 minutes in a day.

4 Five decades is more than 20 000 days

5 There are more than 10 000 hours in one year.

6 What will be the date five weeks after:

a) 10th October   b) 8th June   c) 28th November   d) 26th March?

Look at the calendar for January.

7 On what day will these Saint's Days fall?

a) St. Stephen's Day – December 26th 2003

b) St. Valentine's Day – February 14th 2004

c) St. Andrew's Day – November 30th 2003

d) St. David's Day – March 1st 2004

JANUARY 2004						
Su	M	Tu	W	Th	F	Sa
				1	2	3
4	5	6	7	8	9	10
11	12	13	14	15	16	17
18	19	20	21	22	23	24
25	26	27	28	29	30	31

8 Write out the calendar for March 2004.

9 a) How many complete weeks are there in a year?

b) How many days are left over in a non-leap year?

10 Look at the calendar for January 2004. On what day will fall:

a) January 1st 2003   b) January 1st 2005?

On these pages you will learn to read the time from different clocks.

a.m. means ante meridiem.
It is used for times before noon.
p.m. means post meridiem.
It is used for times after noon.

24-hour clocks always have
four digits on display.
A 24-hour clock displays
midnight as 00:00

Examples

22 minutes past 8   12 minutes to 7

8:22 a.m.   12-hour clock   6:48 p.m.

08:22   24-hour clock   18:48

morning   evening

A

Write each time shown to the nearest minute:

a) in words   b) in 12-hour clock time using a.m. and p.m..

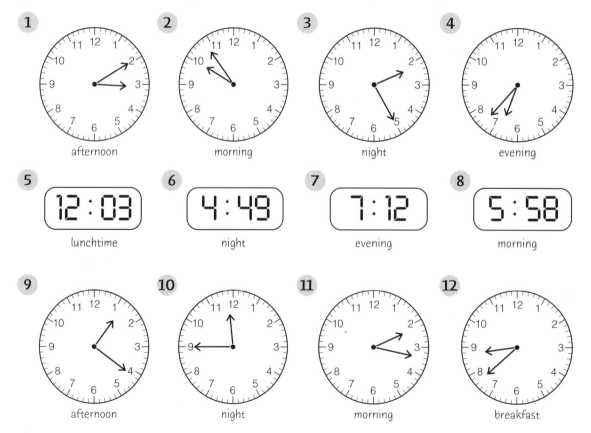

1   **2**   **3**   **4**

afternoon   morning   night   evening

5   **6**   **7**   **8**

| 12:03 | 4:49 | 7:12 | 5:58 |

lunchtime   night   evening   morning

9   **10**   **11**   **12**

afternoon   night   morning   breakfast

13 Write the 12-hour clock times if each of the twelve clocks above was:

a) 9 minutes slow   b) 6 minutes fast.

B

1 Copy and complete the table.

TIME IN WORDS	12-HOUR CLOCK	24-HOUR CLOCK
three o' clock	3:00 p.m.	15:00
		07:45
		20:30
		10:35
		03:52
	10:19 p.m.	
	9:37 a.m.	
	6:16 p.m.	
	11:28 a.m.	
	5:53 p.m.	

2 For each of the above times work out how many minutes there are to the next hour.

3 Write the correct time if each of the above 24-hour clock times is:
a) 35 minutes fast   b) 14 minutes slow.

C

Write each time shown to the nearest minute:
a) in words   b) in 12-hour clock time   c) in 24-hour clock time.

1 morning   2 afternoon   3 night   4 night

5 11:18 morning   6 5:04 afternoon   7 0:37 lunchtime   8 8:33 evening

9 For each of the above times work out how many hours and minutes there are to midnight.

10 Copy and complete the table, changing 12-hour clock times to 24-hour clock times.

	Jan. 2nd	March 6th	May 1st	July 3rd	Sept. 4th	Nov. 6th
Sunrise	8:06 a.m.	6:36 a.m.	5:34 a.m.	4:49 a.m.	6:17 a.m.	7:02 a.m.
Sunset	4:03 p.m.	5:49 p.m.	8:23 p.m.	9:20 p.m.	7:41 p.m.	4:26 p.m.
Daylight length	7 h 57 mins.					

On this page you will learn to use timetables.

Waterloo (London)	07:10	08:35	11:35	13:50
Woking	07:35	–	12:00	14:15
Basingstoke	07:55	09:21	12:21	–
Andover	08:16	–	12:42	–
Salisbury	08:36	09:54	13:17	15:08
Yeovil	09:24	10:42	14:07	15:48
Honiton	10:01	–	14:53	16:34
Exeter	10:27	11:42	15:18	16:59

A

1. How long does it take the 07:10 from Waterloo to travel to:
   a) Woking
   b) Basingstoke
   c) Andover?

2. At how many stations does the 11:35 from Waterloo stop?

3. At what time does the 08:35 from Waterloo reach Salisbury?

4. If you had to be in Exeter by 15:30 which train would you catch from Waterloo?

5. You arrive at Waterloo at 08:20. How long do you have to wait for the next train to Exeter?

6. The 11:35 from Waterloo runs 10 minutes late. At what time will it reach Andover?

B

1. How long does it take the 11:35 from Waterloo to travel to:
   a) Salisbury
   b) Yeovil
   c) Exeter?

2. At how many stations does the 08:16 from Andover stop before it reaches Honiton?

3. At what time does the 12:21 from Basingstoke reach Yeovil?

4. If you had to be in Exeter by 12:00 which train would you catch from Basingstoke?

5. You arrive at Waterloo at 11:08. How long do you have to wait for the next train to Exeter?

6. The 08:35 from Waterloo runs 19 minutes late. At what time will it reach Exeter?

C

1. How long does it take the 07:55 from Basingstoke to travel to:
   a) Salisbury
   b) Yeovil
   c) Exeter?

2. At how many stations does the 09:21 from Basingstoke stop before it reaches Exeter?

3. At what time does the 14:15 from Woking reach Honiton?

4. If you had to be in Honiton by 16:00 which train would you catch from Salisbury?

5. You arrive at Waterloo at 10:42. How long do you have to wait for the next train to Exeter?

6. The 11:35 from Waterloo runs 38 minutes late. At what time will it reach Honiton?

Copy each crossnumber puzzle onto squared paper.
Use the clues to complete the puzzles.

A

1	2		3	4
5		6		
		7	8	
	9		10	11
12			13	

Clues across

1. 9×4
3. $107 - 40$
5. 12.8×10
7. 9×5
10. $42 \div 2$
12. $38 + 19$
13. $200 \div 4$

Clues down

1. $3170 \div 10$
2. 31×2
4. $98 - 21$
6. $58 + 26$
8. $600 - 75$
9. 9×3
11. $100 \div 10$

B

Clues across

1. $502 - 104$ 398
3. 6×9 63
5. $82 - 24$
6. 76.2×10 762
7. $316 + 46$ 302
11. 0.43×100 43
13. 41×5 205
15. $963 - 71$ 892
16. $150 \div 2$ 75

Clues down

1. 0.35×100 35
2. $633 + 350$ 983
3. $112 \div 2$ 56
4. $387 + 39$ 426
6. 12×6 72
8. 8^2 64
9. $296 - 48$ 248
10. $3001 - 2894$ 107
12. $124 - 85$
14. $5500 \div 100$

1	2			3	4
5			6		
	7	8			
9				10	
11	12		13		14
15				16	

C

1	2	3		4	5
6				7	
	8		9		
10			11	12	
13	14				
15			16		

Clues across

1. 8×59
4. 13×7
6. $1002 - 18$
7. $300 \div 5$
8. $6080 \div 10$
11. $1000 - 251$
13. 9.24×100
15. $1000 \div 20$
16. 11^2

Clues down

1. $196 \div 4$
2. $689 + 97$
3. 20×12
4. $9600 \div 100$
5. $4003 - 2994$
9. $174 \div 2$
10. 79×5
12. $385 + 57$
14. $320 \div 16$

On these pages you will learn to use co-ordinates to find the position of a point on a grid.

The position of a point on a grid is given by its *x* and *y* co-ordinates.

Examples

The position of point A.
Start at the origin, (0, 0).
Go across 4 along the x-axis.
Go up 2 along the y-axis.
Point A is (4, 2).

Point B is (2, 4).
Across 2 along the x-axis.
Up 4 along the y-axis.

Remember: The x co-ordinate always comes first.

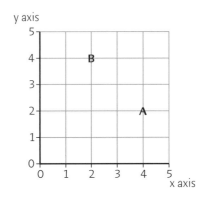

A

1 Use the grid below to work out the joke written in co-ordinates.
Work *down* each column.

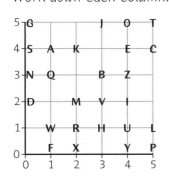

(1,1)	(4,0)	(1,4)	(1,1)	(0,4)	(0,2)
(3,1)	(4,5)		(4,2)	(5,0)	(4,5)
(1,4)	(4,1)	(2,2)	(5,5)	(1,4)	(4,1)
(5,5)		(1,4)	(3,1)	(0,2)	(0,5)
		(5,4)	(0,3)		(4,4)
(0,2)	(1,4)			(1,4)	
(4,5)	(5,1)				
	(5,1)				

2 Draw a 5 × 5 grid.
Plot the points for shape A.
Join them up in the order given.
Use a different colour for each shape.

A	B	C	D
(2,1)	(0,3)	(0,0)	(5,2)
(3,4)	(0,5)	(0,2)	(5,4)
(4,1)	(2,5)	(5,0)	(1,4)
(2,1)	(2,3)	(0,0)	(1,2)
	(0,3)		(5,2)

3 Use the grid in question 1 to write the name of:
a) your teacher.
b) your favourite colour.
c) a pop group.
d) a football team.

B

1 Draw a 10 × 10 grid.
Plot the points in the first column.
Join them up in the order given.
You should have drawn a letter.

Do the same for the other columns
using the same grid.

(4,6) (2,5) (7,1) (10,7)
(4,10) (2,6) (7,4) (9,8)
(6,10) (0,6) (5,4) (8,7)
(6,8) (0,2) (5,0) (10,5)
(4,8) (2,2) (7,0) (9,4)
(6,6) (2,3) (7,1) (8,5)
       (3,3) (8,0)

2 Use the grid below to work out the message written in co-ordinates?
Work *down* each column.

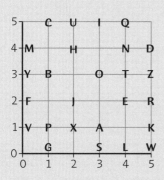

(5,0) (0,3) (1,3) (2,1) (1,5)
(2,4)   (4,2)   (5,2)
(0,3) (1,0) (1,5) (3,5) (3,3)
       (3,3) (3,1) (3,0) (3,0)
(5,4)   (2,5)   (3,0)
(3,3) (2,5) (3,0) (3,1)
(4,2) (1,1) (4,2)
(3,0)   ?

C

1 Use the grid below to work out the joke written in co-ordinates.
Work *across* each row.

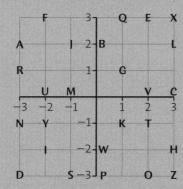

(0,−2) (3,−2) (−3,2) (2,−1) (−3,−3) (2,−3)
(−2,−1) (2,−3) (−2,0)
(3,0) (−3,2) (3,2) (3,2) (−3,2) (2,−3) (−3,−1) (2,3)
(2,3) (−2,−1) (2,3) (−3,−3)
(−3,−3) (−2,−2) (−3,−1) (2,−3)
 (−1,−3) (−3,2) (−2,0) (−3,1)?
(−3,−3) (2,−3) (−2,−1) (2,−3) (−2,0) (2,−1) (3,−2)
 (−2,−2) (−3,−1) (1,−1) (2,−1) (3,−2)
(2,3) (−2,−1) (−1,−3) (−3,2)
 (−2,0) (−3,1) (−2,0) (−1,−3).

2 Draw a grid like the one above.
Plot the points for Shape A and join them up in the given order.
Use a different colour for each shape. Can you name each of the shapes?

A	B	C	D
(−3,−2)	(−1,−1)	(3,−1)	(−1,1)
(−1,2)	(−2,1)	(−3,1)	(1,−1)
(3,0)	(2,3)	(−1,3)	(−1,−3)
	(3,1)		(−3,−1)

3 Now use the grid above to write your own joke in co-ordinates.

On these pages you will learn:

- **to recognise parallel and perpendicular lines.**

Parallel lines are lines that are the same distance apart for all their length. Railway lines are parallel lines.

Perpendicular lines cross or meet at right angles.

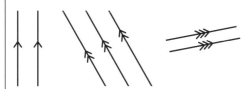

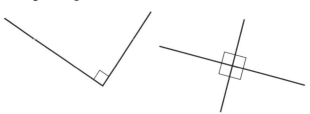

- **to recognise diagonal lines.**

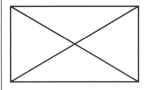

Diagonal lines go from one vertex (corner) of a shape to another.

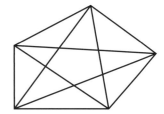

A

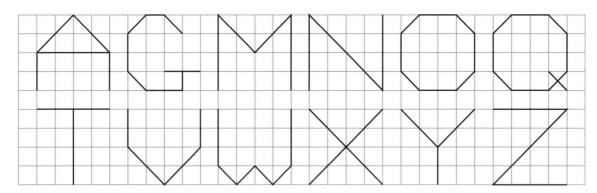

1. How many pairs of parallel lines does each of the above letters have?

2. Which of the letters do not have perpendicular lines?

3. The diagonals of a square have the following properties:
   a) they are equal in length.
   b) they bisect each other (cut each other in half).
   c) they are perpendicular.

   Draw round templates of quadrilaterals.
   Investigate the diagonals for these three properties.

   Use squared paper. Try to draw other irregular quadrilaterals with at least one of these three properties.

B

1. Use squared paper.
   Copy out each of the letters in Section A in a 4 × 4 grid.
   Show all the parallel lines with coloured pens or pencils.
   Use a different colour for each pair of parallel lines in a letter. Show all the perpendicular lines by marking a right angle.

2. Draw round a template of a regular hexagon (or trace the diagram.)
   Now draw on all the diagonals.
   a) How many diagonals are there?
   b) What do you notice about the length of the diagonals?
   c) Where do three of the diagonals meet?

   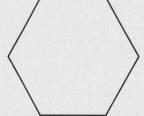

3. Investigate the diagonals of irregular hexagons.
   Do you get the same results as for regular hexagons?

4. Now investigate the diagonals of other polygons, both regular and irregular.

C

1. Use squared paper.
   Draw an irregular hexagon with:
   a) 2 pairs of parallel lines   c) 3 pairs of perpendicular lines
   b) 3 pairs of parallel lines   d) 4 pairs of perpendicular lines.

2. Copy and complete this table.

   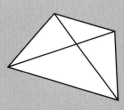

Shape	Number of diagonals
quadrilateral	
pentagon	
hexagon	
heptagon	
octagon	

   Can you see a pattern?

   Without drawing the shape work out how many diagonals there would be in a shape with:
   a) 9 sides   c) 11 sides
   b) 10 sides   d) 12 sides.

3. Investigate the largest number of parallel lines you can draw with different polygons.

4. Investigate the largest number of perpendicular lines you can draw with different polygons.

On these pages you will learn to classify 2-D shapes.

2-D shapes with straight lines are called *polygons*.
(Equal lines are shown with dashes and equal angles are marked.)

A three-sided polygon is a *triangle*.

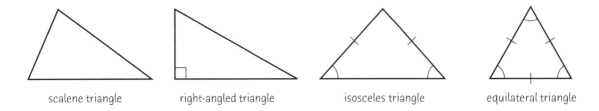

scalene triangle   right-angled triangle   isosceles triangle   equilateral triangle

A four-sided polygon is a *quadrilateral*.

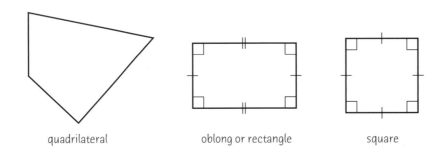

quadrilateral   oblong or rectangle   square

OTHER POLYGONS   5 sides – pentagon   7 sides – heptagon
                        6 sides – hexagon   8 sides – octagon

REGULAR POLYGONS   IRREGULAR POLYGONS

All sides and   Sides and angles
all angles are equal.   are not all equal.

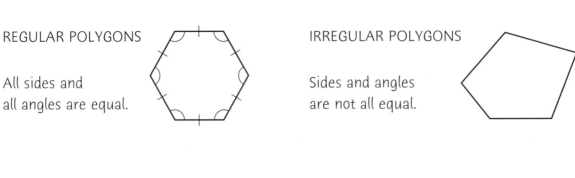

CONCAVE POLYGONS   CONVEX POLYGONS

One angle greater   No angle greater
than 180°   than 180°

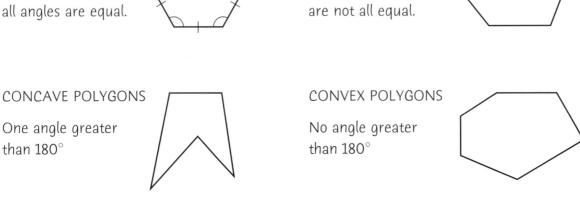

Here are some shapes.

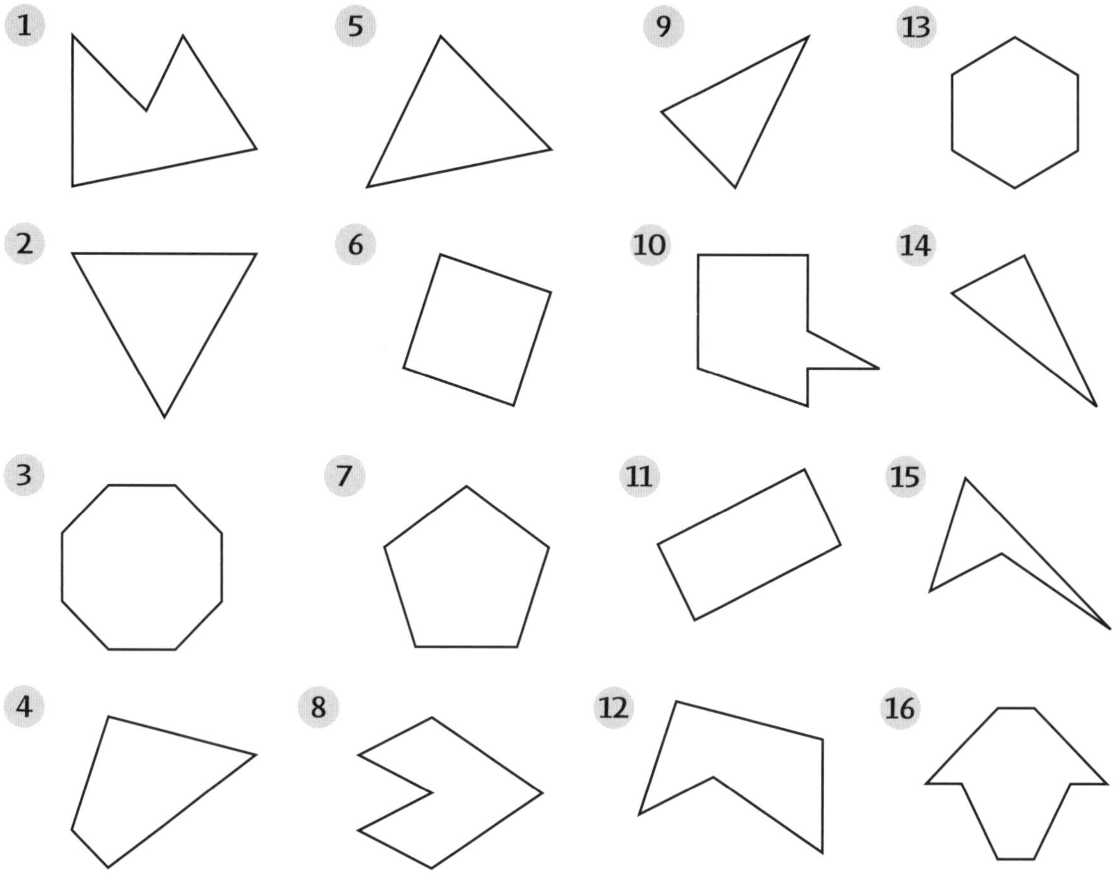

1

5

9

13

2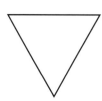

6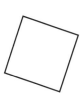

10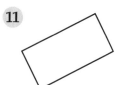

14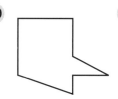

3

7

11

15

4

8

12

16

A

1 Write the name of each of the above shapes (e.g. square, regular pentagon, etc.).

2 Which of the shapes are concave?

3 Draw a concave octagon.

B

Copy and complete the table for each of the above shapes.

Number	Name of shape	No. of sides	Equal sides	Equal angles
1	irregular pentagon	5	2	2

C

1 Which of the above shapes have pairs of parallel lines?
How many pairs of parallel lines does each shape have?

2 Use squared paper.
On a 3 × 3 grid (9 small squares) draw three different examples of:
a) isosceles triangles
b) squares
c) right-angled triangles
d) scalene triangles
e) quadrilaterals
f) pentagons
g) hexagons
h) heptagons.

On these pages you will learn to classify 3-D shapes according to their properties.

Some 3-D shapes with curved faces.

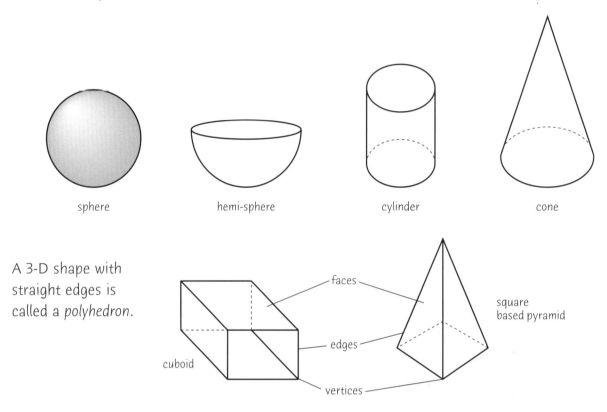

sphere   hemi-sphere   cylinder   cone

A 3-D shape with straight edges is called a *polyhedron*.

faces

cuboid

edges

vertices

square based pyramid

Regular polyhedra have faces which are identical.

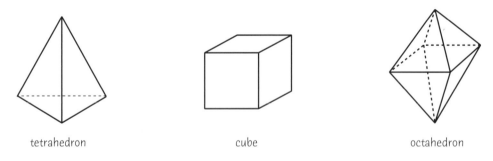

tetrahedron   cube   octahedron

A *prism* is a polyhedron with two identical end faces and the same cross section throughout its length.

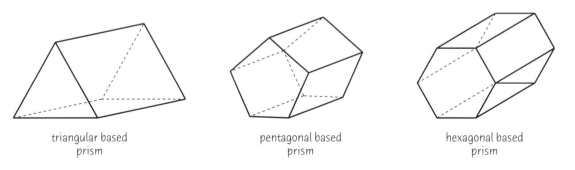

triangular based prism   pentagonal based prism   hexagonal based prism

Here are some shapes.

1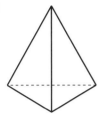

5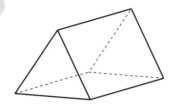

9

2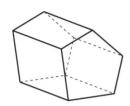

6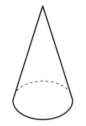

10

3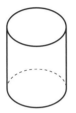

7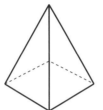

11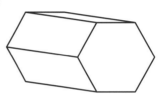

4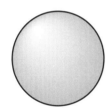

8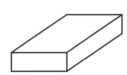

12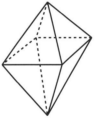

A

1 Write down the name of each of the above shapes.

2 Sort the shapes into the following groups.

  a) shapes with curved faces   c) prisms

  b) regular polyhedra   d) shapes with five flat faces

B

Copy and complete the table for each of the shapes.

No.	Shape	Faces	Edges	Vertices
1	tetrahedron	4	6	4

C

Describe the flat faces for each of the shapes.

Example

5 triangular prism   2 triangles   3 rectangles

On this page you will investigate different ways of making polygons.

In the following problems you will be drawing different shapes. Each shape should be different, not the same shape in a different position.

These quadrilaterals are the same,
Make sure that all of your shapes are different.

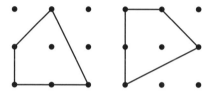

A

1   Use dotty paper or squared paper.   **Examples**
    Draw different triangles on a 3 × 3 grid.
    There are eight different triangles altogether.
    Can you find them all?

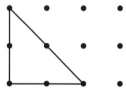

2   Label each of your triangles – scalene, isosceles or right-angled.

3   The area of the grid is 4 squares.
    The triangles in the examples have areas of 2 squares and 1 square.
    Work out the areas of each of your triangles.

B

This square on a 3 × 3 grid has an area of 2 squares.
It is half the area of the grid, which is 4 squares.

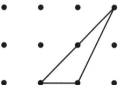

1   On a 4 × 4 grid, draw a square with an area of 5 squares.

2   On a 5 × 5 grid, draw a square with an area of 10 squares.

3   These two squares have been drawn on a 5 × 5 grid.
    Eight different squares can be drawn altogether.
    Can you find them all?

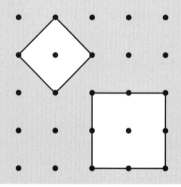

C

1   There are 11 different squares you can make on a 6 × 6 grid. Try to find them all.
    (A 6 × 6 grid has 25 small squares.)

2   Now explore a 7 × 7 grid. Good luck!

On this page you will learn to make nets for 3-D shapes.

A

Which of these nets will make an open cube?

         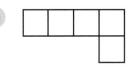

1   **2**   **3**   **4**

Copy the nets onto squared paper. Cut them out and see if you were right.

There are 8 different nets for an open cube. Find as many as you can.

B

1 Copy this net onto squared paper.
Cut it out and make the cuboid.

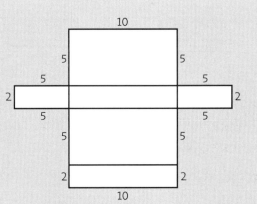

2 Make nets for these cuboids.

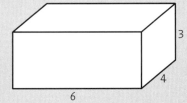   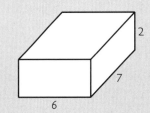

C

1 Copy this net onto squared paper.
Cut it out and make the pyramid.

2 Use triangle dotty paper.
Make this net for a tetrahedron.

Can you find a different net that
makes a tetrahedron?

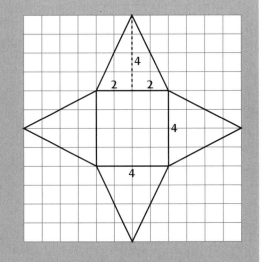

On this page you will learn to visualise 3-D shapes from 2-D drawings.

1

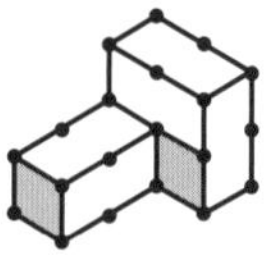

6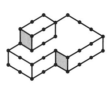

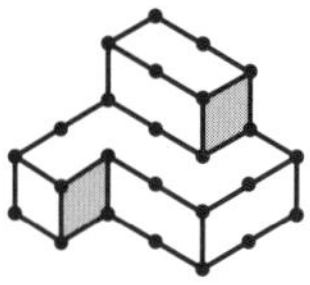

11

2

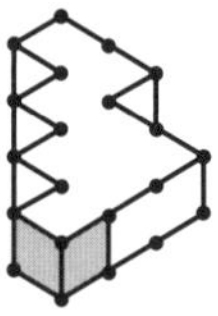

7

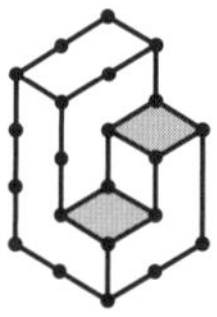

12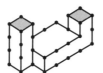

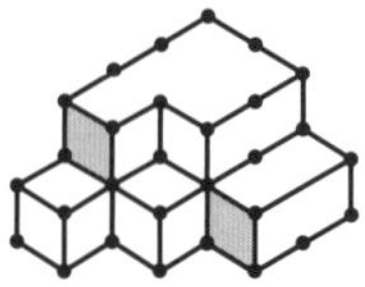

3

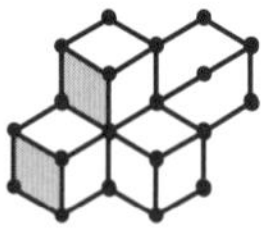

8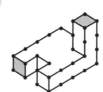

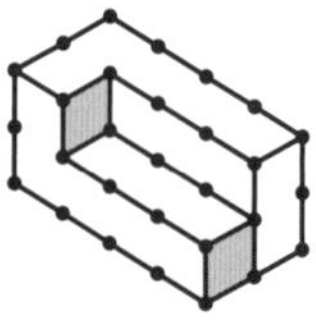

13

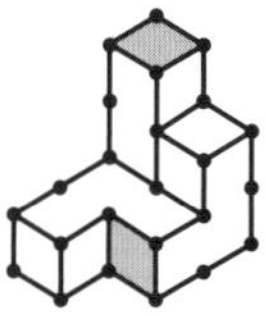

4

9

14

5

10

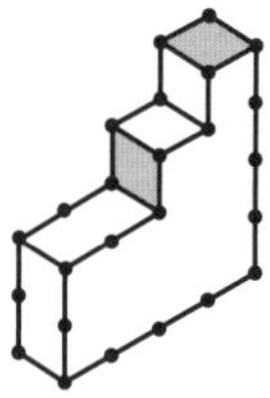

15

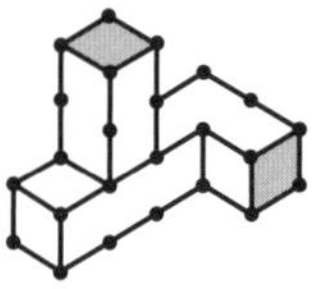

A

How many cubes are needed to build these shapes?

B

How many more cubes are needed to turn each shape into a cuboid?

Examples

Number 1   Six cubes are needed.
Number 2   Eight cubes are needed.

C

What is the least number of cubes needed to cover and join the two shaded faces?

Examples

Number 1   Four cubes are needed.
Number 2   Three cubes are needed.

On this page you will learn to recognise reflective symmetry in 2-D shapes.

A shape is symmetrical if half of its shape matches the other half exactly.
The line separating the two halves is the line of symmetry or mirror line.

Examples

One line
of symmetry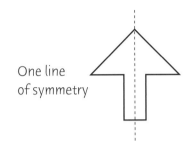

Two lines
of symmetry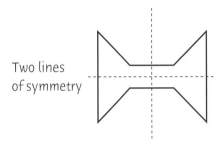

Draw around templates of different triangles and quadrilaterals (or trace the shapes on page 96).
Draw on the lines of symmetry.

B

Draw round the templates of different regular polygons (or trace the shapes on page 97).
Draw on the lines of symmetry.

Copy and complete the table.

Shape	No. of sides	No. of lines of symmetry
equilateral triangle		
square		
regular pentagon		
regular hexagon		
regular octagon		

Investigate the lines of symmetry in irregular polygons.

Examples

Can you draw an irregular hexagon with:
a) no lines of symmetry
b) one line of symmetry
c) two lines of symmetry
d) more than two lines of symmetry?

Can you draw an irregular octagon with:
a) one line of symmetry
b) two lines of symmetry
c) three lines of symmetry
d) four lines of symmetry?

On this page you will learn to sketch the reflection of a shape in a mirror line.

Examples

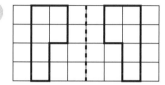

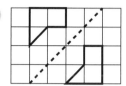

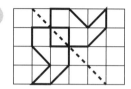

Copy the shape and the mirror line and sketch the reflection.

A

1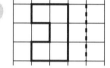

2

3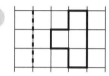

4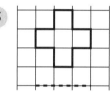

5

6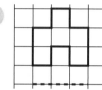

7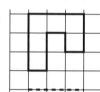

8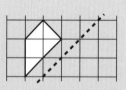

B

1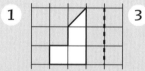

2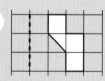

3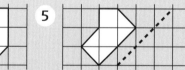

4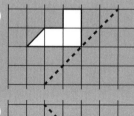

5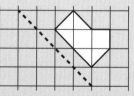

6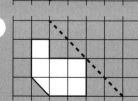

7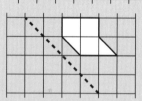

8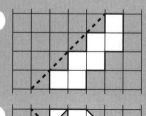

C

1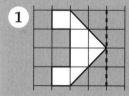

2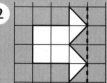

3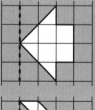

4

5

6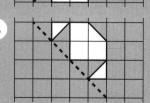

On this page you will learn to complete symmetrical patterns with one or two lines of symmetry.

Examples

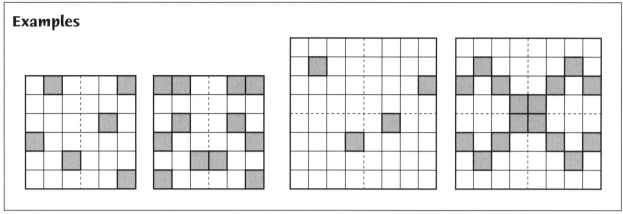

Copy the patterns below on squared paper.

Shade in as many squares as necessary to complete the symmetrical patterns.

A

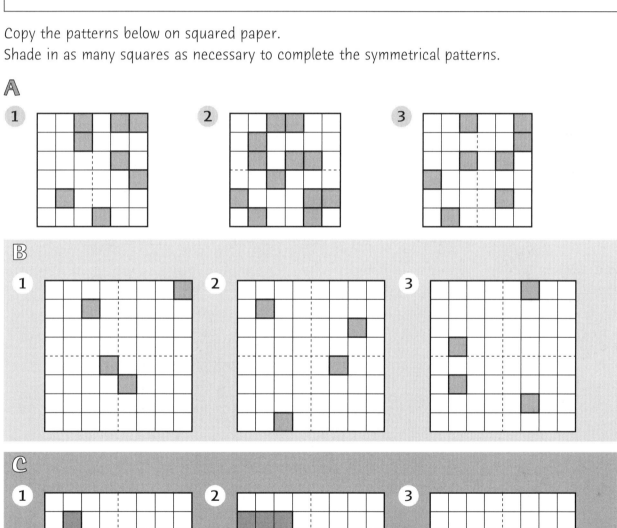

B

1 2 3

C

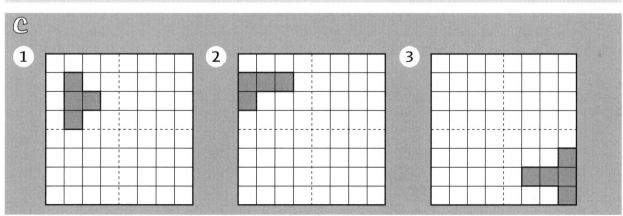

1 2 3

On this page you will learn to sketch the pattern of a shape after it has been translated.

Translating a shape means moving it in a straight line.

Examples Translate the shaded shape:

1 left 3 squares (L3) **3** Right 2 Up 2 (R2 U2)

2 up 2 squares (U2) **4** Right 2 Down 1 (R2 D1).

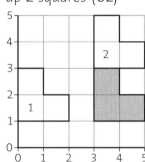 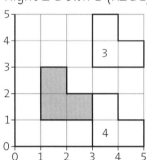

 A

Investigate making patterns by repeatedly translating a shape in a horizontal line:

a) one square b) two squares c) half a square.

Examples

Use these shapes or make up your own.

B

Copy the grids and the shaded shapes. Translate each shape three times.

1 U2 **4** L2
2 R3 **5** R2
3 D2 **6** U3

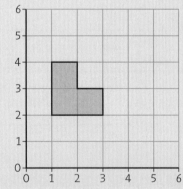 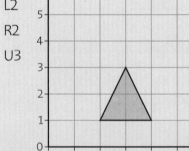

C

1 Copy the grid and the L-shaped hexagon in Section B. Translate the shape three times.
a) L1 D2 b) R3 D1 c) R1 U2

2 Copy the grid and the triangle in Section B. Translate the shape three times.
a) L1 U2 b) R2 D1 c) R2 U3

3 Make up your own examples.

On these pages you will learn to estimate, measure and draw angles accurately.

Angles measure the amount something turns or rotates. Angles are measured in degrees (°).

A whole turn
360°

A right angle
90°

An acute angle
Less than 90°

An obtuse angle
Greater than 90° and
less than 180°

USING A PROTRACTOR

A protractor is used to measure or draw angles accurately. Most protractors have two scales, a clockwise outer scale and an anti-clockwise inner scale.
It is important to use the correct scale.

Examples

Outer Scale

$A\widehat{O}B = 50°$

$A\widehat{O}C = 140°$

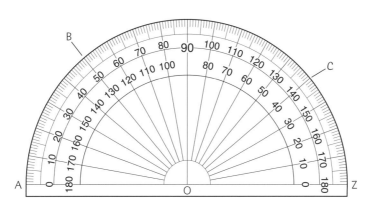

Inner Scale

$Z\widehat{O}C = 40°$

$Z\widehat{O}B = 130°$

COMMON MISTAKES

1 Using the wrong scale.
Before measuring, decide if the angle is greater than or less than 90°.

2 Reading the scale in the wrong direction.
The angle in the example is 125° but could be read wrongly as 135°.
Make sure you look at the numbers on both sides of the line.

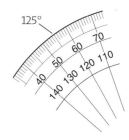

125°

108

A

Decide which is the correct angle from the two answers.
Do *not* measure the angles.

1  **3**  **5**  **7**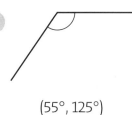

(70°, 110°)   (60°, 120°)   (80°, 100°)   (55°, 125°)

2  **4**  **6**   **8**

(50°, 130°)   (40°, 140°)   (30°, 150°)   (85°, 95°)

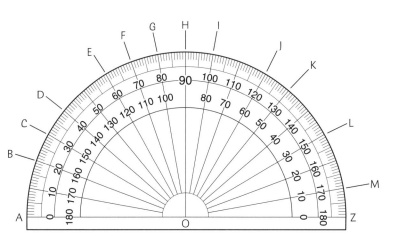

Look at the protractor. Give the measurement of each angle.

Use the outer scale.   Use the inner scale.

9 AÔE   **13** AÔB   **17** AÔG   **21** ZÔL   **25** ZÔK   **29** ZÔH

10 AÔC   **14** AÔH   **18** AÔK   **22** ZÔI   **26** ZÔB   **30** ZÔD

11 AÔI   **15** AÔD   **19** AÔF   **23** ZÔF   **27** ZÔM   **31** ZÔJ

12 AÔM   **16** AÔL   **20** AÔJ   **24** ZÔC   **28** ZÔE   **32** ZÔG

Use a protractor to draw the following angles.
Write acute or obtuse by each angle.

33 30°   **34** 100°   **35** 10°   **36** 150°   **37** 60°   **38** 160°

For each of these angles:

a) identify whether it is an acute angle or an obtuse angle.

b) estimate the size of the angle to the nearest 10°.

c) measure the angle to the nearest 10°.

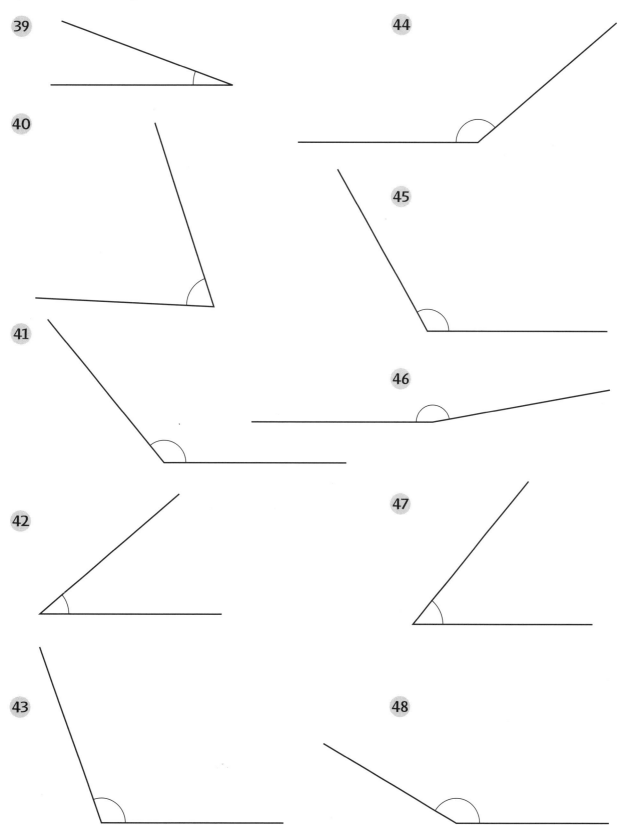

B

State whether the following angles are acute or obtuse.
Do not measure the angles

1

3

5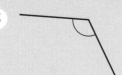

7

2

4

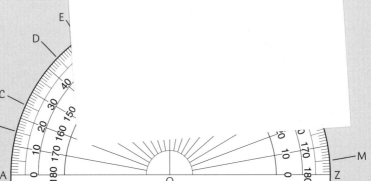

×12 − 5D

×8 − 5R

Give the measurement of each angle to the nearest 5°.

Use the outer scale.　　　　　　　　　　Use the inner scale.

9 AÔD　　**13** AÔB　　**17** AÔI　　**21** ZÔL　　**25** ZÔK　　**29** ZÔH

10 AÔL　　**14** AÔH　　**18** AÔK　　**22** ZÔI　　**26** ZÔB　　**30** ZÔD

11 AÔG　　**15** AÔE　　**19** AÔF　　**23** ZÔF　　**27** ZÔM　　**31** ZÔJ

12 AÔM　　**16** AÔC　　**20** AÔJ　　**24** ZÔC　　**28** ZÔE　　**32** ZÔG

Use a protractor to draw the following angles.
Write acute or obtuse by each angle.

33 45°　　**34** 145°　　**35** 25°　　**36** 125°　　**37** 75°　　**38** 155°

39 Draw a triangle with angles of 90° and 40°.
Measure the third angle. What is the sum of the three angles?

40 Draw a quadrilateral with angles of 90°, 90° and 110°.
Measure the fourth angle. What is the sum of the four angles?

For each of these angles:
a) identify whether it is an acute angle or an obtuse angle.
b) estimate the size of the angle to the nearest 5°.
c) measure the angle to the nearest 5°.

41

42

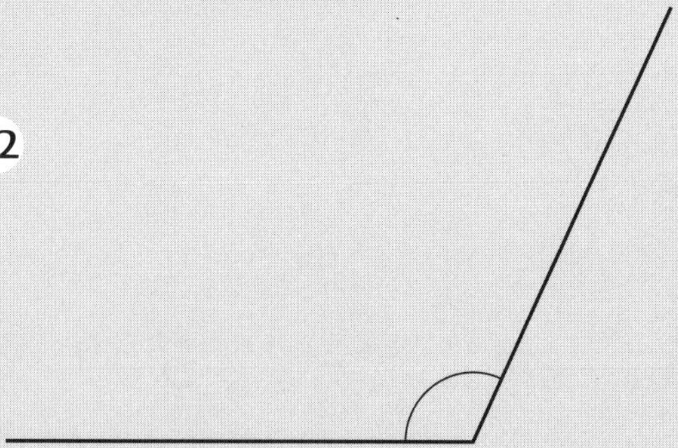

43

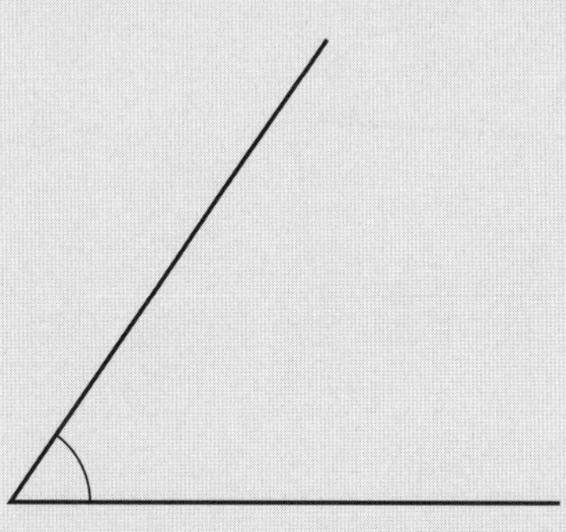

44

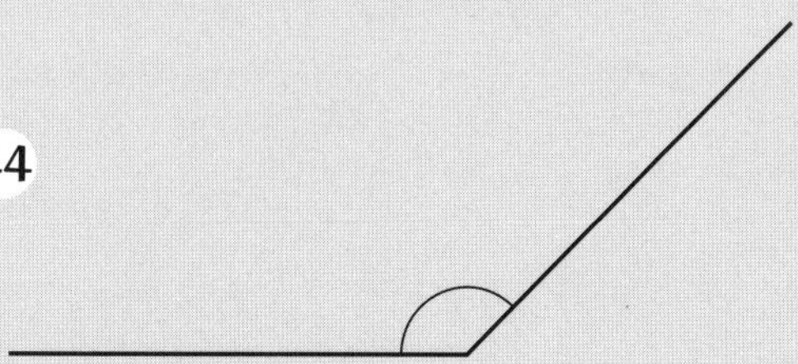

45

46

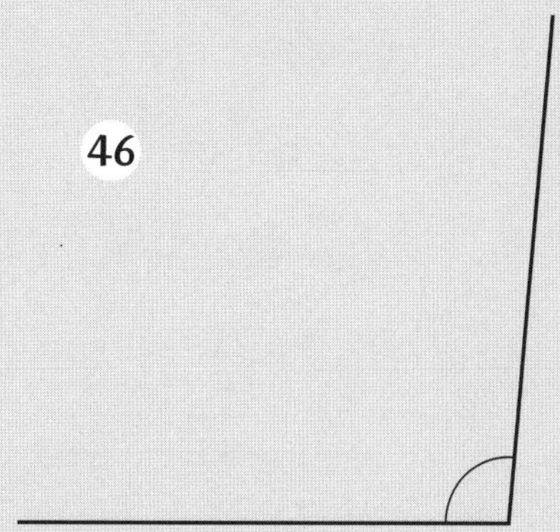

47

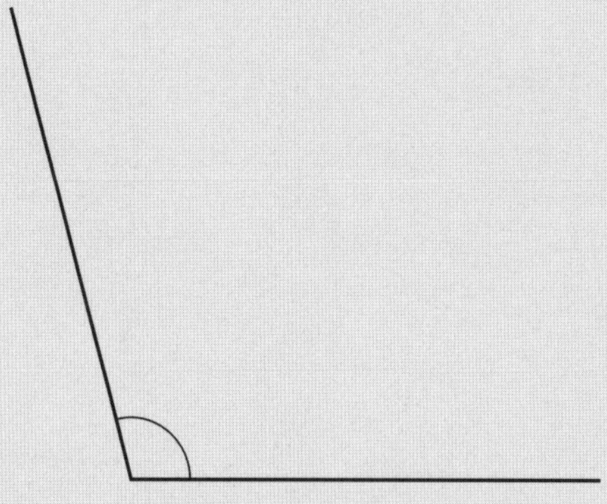

48

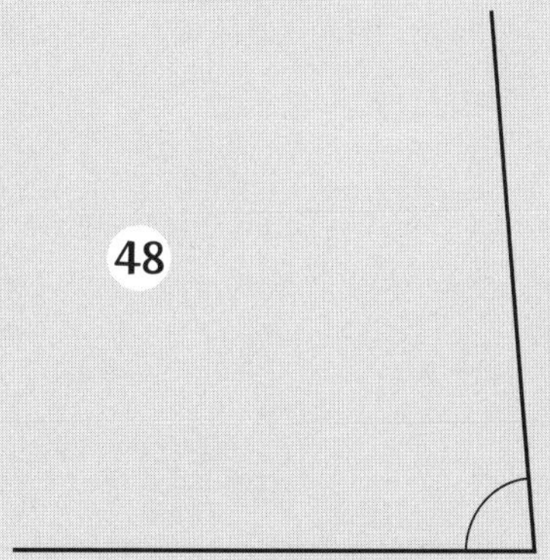

49

50

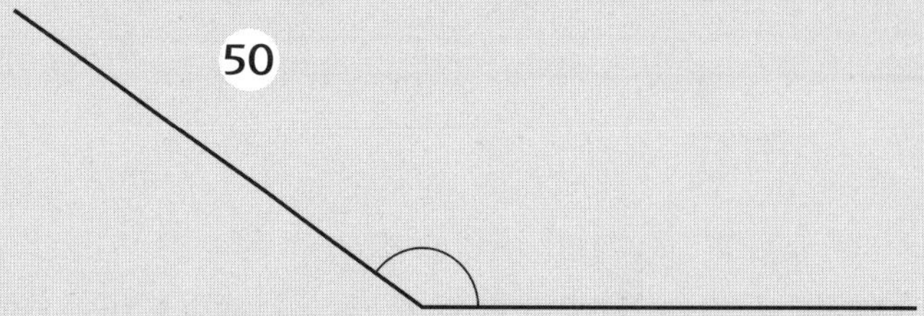

C

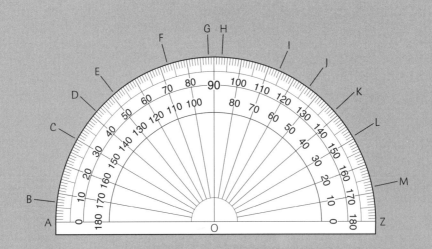

Look at the protractor. Give the measurement of each angle.

1	AÔE	**5**	AÔI	**9**	AÔH	**13**	ZÔM	**17**	ZÔH	**21**	ZÔK
2	ZÔL	**6**	ZÔF	**10**	ZÔJ	**14**	AÔJ	**18**	AÔK	**22**	AÔL
3	AÔC	**7**	AÔM	**11**	AÔB	**15**	ZÔE	**19**	ZÔC	**23**	ZÔB
4	ZÔI	**8**	ZÔD	**12**	ZÔG	**16**	AÔF	**20**	AÔG	**24**	AÔD

Estimate the size of these angles.

25 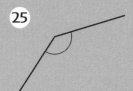　　**27** 　　**29** 　　**31**

26 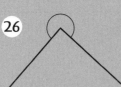　　**28** 　　**30** 　　**32**

33 a) Draw five different triangles.
　　b) Measure the angles.
　　c) Work out the sum of the angles for each triangle. What do you notice?

34 Work out the sum of the angles of a rectangle.
　　Now investigate the sum of the angles of other quadrilaterals.
　　(You may find it helpful to measure the angles of templates.)

On this page you will learn to calculate angles in a straight line.

Example

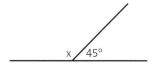

$$x° + 45° = 180°$$
$$x° = 135°$$

A

Calculate the missing angles.

1 150° a

3 c 80°

5 65° e

7 g 55°

2 110° b

4 d 60°

6 125° f

8 h 95°

B

Calculate the missing angles.

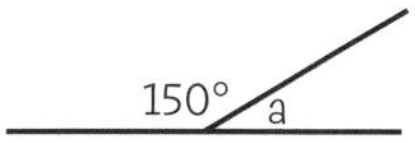

1 75° i

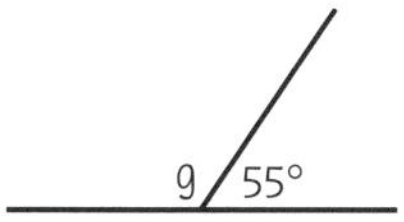

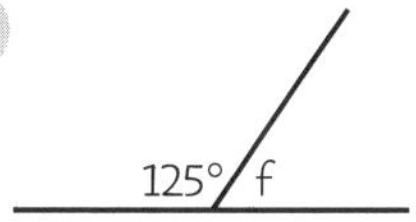

3 k 48°

5 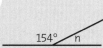 59° m

7 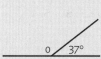 o 37°

2 136° j

4 l 142°

6 154° n

8 p 113°

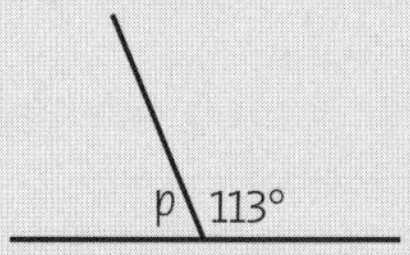

C

Calculate the missing angles.

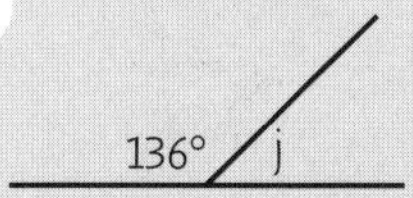

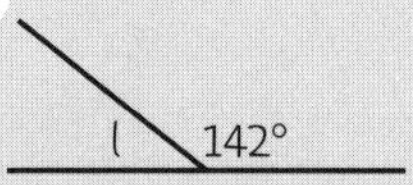

1 60° 80° q

3 s 64° 70°

5 73° u

7 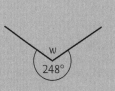 w 248°

2 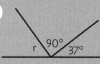 r 90° 37°

4 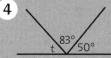 83° t 50°

6 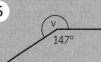 v 147°

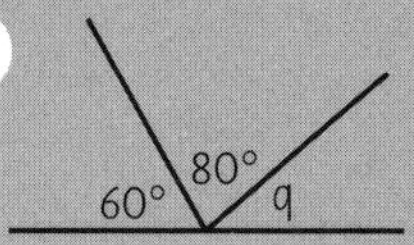

8 128° x 128°

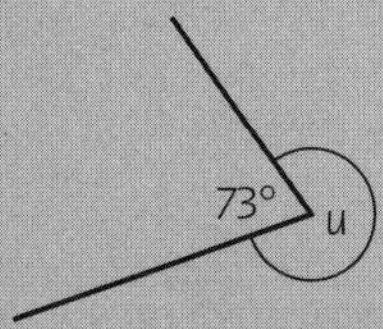

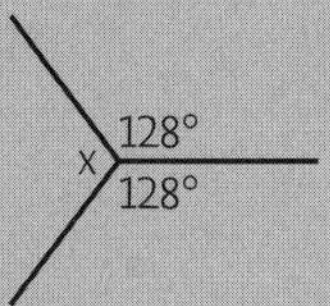

On these pages you will learn to use the language associated with probability.

The probability of something happening is the likelihood or chance that it might happen.

Examples

What is the probability of these events?

1   The sun will rise tomorrow.

2   You will live to be 500.

3   You spin a coin and get a head.

4   It will rain tomorrow.

5   You will see a bus on your way home.

6   You will see an ambulance on your way home.

The probabilities of these events can be placed on a scale. You might choose to place them in these positions. Numbers 1 to 3 could not be put anywhere else but the last three statements depend upon the circumstances.

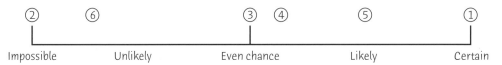

②	⑥		③ ④		⑤		①
Impossible	Unlikely		Even chance		Likely		Certain

 A

For each of these statements write one of these probabilities.

certain   likely   even chance   unlikely   impossible

1   You will get married next week.

2   You will watch television this evening.

3   The next match a football team play will be a home game.

4   Your teacher will win the Lottery and retire to the Bahamas.

5   You will have a birthday in the next year.

6   You roll a dice and get a 6.

7   The phone will ring this evening.

8   You will have a new pair of shoes in the next three months.

9   You will learn to juggle in the next year.

10   It will snow next week.

B

Discuss the probability of these events.
Place them on a scale like the one on the previous page.

1 You will get married when you grow up.

2 The Queen was born on a Thursday.

3 Someone in the family will receive a letter tomorrow.

4 You will pass your driving test next year.

5 You roll a dice and get an even number.

6 The next person to come into the classroom will be the Headteacher.

7 A baby will be born somewhere in the world today.

8 Everyone in the class will watch television next week.

9 Your television set will need to be repaired in the next five years.

10 A teacher at your school will have a Number 1 hit record.

11 Place the ten events in Section A on a new scale.

C

Work out these probabilities as a fraction and place each on this scale.

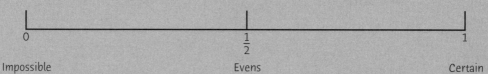

1 Rolling a dice and getting a 6.

2 Rolling a dice and getting a 7.

3 Rolling a dice and getting a number less than 5.

4 Drawing a card from a pack and getting a diamond.

5 Drawing a card from a pack and getting a black card.

6 Drawing a card from a pack and getting an ace.

7 Drawing a card from a pack and not getting a club.

8 Spinning a coin and getting a head.

9 Spinning a coin and getting a tail or a head.

10 Spinning two coins and getting two heads.

On these pages you will learn to find the range and mode of a set of data and to interpret bar charts and bar line charts.

RANGE
The range is how far it is from the highest value to the lowest value.

MODE
The mode is the most common value.

Example

This bar line chart shows the lengths of the stories written by 30 children.

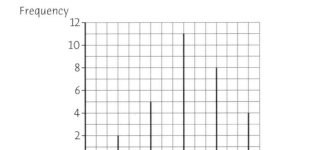

Longest stories	5 pages
Shortest stories	1 page
Range of lengths	$5 - 1 = 4$ pages
Modal length	3 pages

1 This bar chart shows the takings of a burger stall during one week.

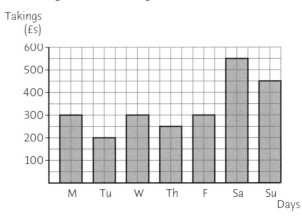

a) What was the maximum daily taking?
b) What was the minimum daily taking?
c) What was the range of the takings?
d) Why do you think takings were greatest on Saturday and Sunday?

2 This bar line chart shows the destinations of holidays sold by a travel agent.

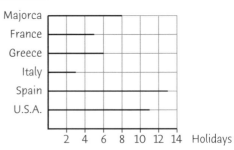

a) How many holidays were sold to the U.S.A.?
b) Which was the most popular destination?
c) Which was the least popular destination?
d) How many more holidays were sold to Majorca than to France?
e) How many holidays were sold altogether during the week?

B

1 This bar chart shows the marks Jason achieved in his weekly spelling test.

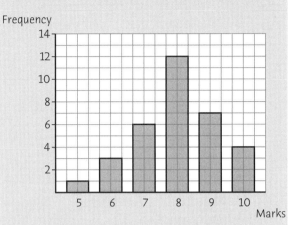

a) What was Jason's highest score?
b) What was his lowest score?
c) What was the range of his scores?
d) What was Jason's modal score?
e) How many times did Jason score less than 8?

2 This bar line chart shows how many times each number was thrown when a dice was rolled repeatedly.

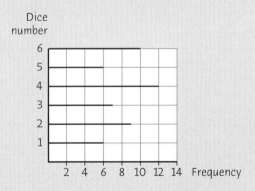

a) Which dice score was the mode?
b) How many times was 2 rolled?
c) How many more times was 6 rolled than 1?
d) How many times was a number less than 3 rolled?
e) How many times was an even number rolled?
f) How many times was the dice rolled altogether?

C

1 This bar chart shows the number of goals scored by entrants in a penalty competition.

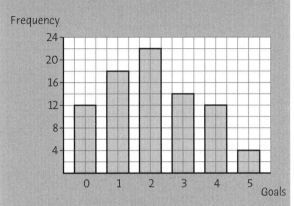

a) What was the highest number of goals scored?
b) What was the modal number of goals scored?
c) How many competitors scored more than 2 goals?
d) How many competitors scored less than 2 goals?
e) How many people took part in the competition?
f) How many goals were scored altogether?

2 Roll two dice. Add the scores to give a total.
Repeat this 50 times keeping a tally of the total scores.
Draw a bar line chart to show the results.
What was the range of scores?
Which dice score was the mode?
Did this surprise you?

On these pages you will learn to draw and interpret line graphs.

Line graphs are graphs in which a set of data is plotted and the points are joined up with a line. Line graphs often show a trend.

Example

This line graph shows the average daily maximum temperature in London during the year.

Month	J F M A M J J A S O N D
Temperature (°C)	4 5 7 9 12 16 18 17 15 11 8 5

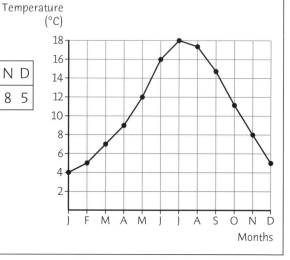

A

Match each of these statements to one of the graphs.

1. The temperature rises steadily.

2. The temperature begins to rise and then falls quickly.

3. The temperature rises more and more quickly.

4. The temperature stays the same and then falls quickly.

5. The temperature falls faster and faster.

6. The temperature rises, stays the same and then rises quickly.

7. The table shows the results of Sara's weekly tables test. Use the data to draw a line graph. Remember to label the axes.

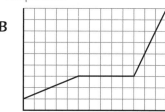

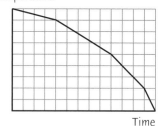

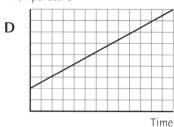

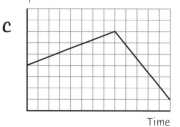

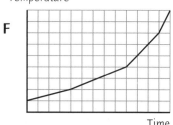

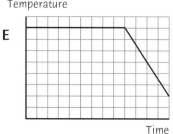

Week	1	2	3	4	5	6	7	8	9	10
Mark	3	4	5	6	5	6	6	7	8	9

B

1 This line graph shows the depth of
water in a stream throughout the year.

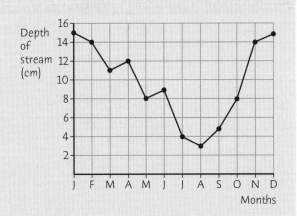

a) How deep was the stream in March?

b) In which two months was the stream
8 cm deep?

c) Which month saw the largest increase
in depth? Why do you think this
happened?

d) What was the range of the depths?

2 Use the table below to draw a line graph showing the temperature in a room in a school
over 24 hours. Remember to label the axes.

Time	0400	0600	0800	1000	1200	1400	1600	1800	2000	2200	0000	0200	0400
Room temperature (°C)	3	2	14	18	19	19	17	14	8	5	5	4	3

a) What was the range in temperature in the room during the day?

b) When did the temperature increase most rapidly? Why do you think this happened?

C

1 This line graph shows the average daily
temperature in Sweden.

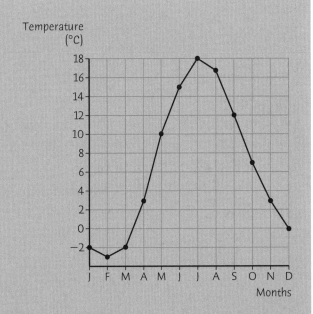

a) What was the temperature in June?

b) In which month was the
temperature 7°C?

c) In which two months was the
temperature 3°C?

d) Which two months saw the largest fall
in temperature?

e) What was the range of temperature
over the year?

2 Use the table to draw a line graph to show the improvement in an athlete's time for
running 400 m. You will need to use graph paper.

Week	1	2	3	4	5	6	7	8	9	10	11	12
400 m time (seconds)	58·6	58·2	57·3	56·9	56·1	55·5	54·6	54·9	53·5	53·1	52·9	52·8

a) In which week did she make the greatest improvement in time?

b) In which week do you think she had a slight cold?

Write in words.

1 75 240

2 320 108

3 1 407 850

4 2 090 016

Give the value of the underlined digit.

5 129 417

6 1 583 000

7 45 936

8 3 506 200

Work out

9 249 × 10

10 3000 × 10

11 4180 × 10

12 37 × 100

13 1500 × 100

14 461 × 100

15 42 000 ÷ 10

16 300 000 ÷ 10

17 6020 ÷ 10

18 23 000 ÷ 100

19 58 600 ÷ 100

20 200 000 ÷ 100

Use these digits.

6   9   2   5

21 Make the largest possible number.

22 Make the smallest possible number.

B

Round to the nearest 100.

23 863

25 2970

24 1247

26 4652

Round to the nearest 1000.

27 7394

29 26 298

28 14 516

30 19 730

Approximate by rounding to the nearest 10.

31 462 + 87

32 536 + 243

33 86 − 38

34 162 − 93

35 39 × 5

36 48 × 7

37 What number is shown by each arrow?

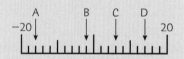

Look at the number line above. What is the difference between:

38 A and B   **40** C and A

39 B and C   **41** D and B?

42 Write in order, smallest first.

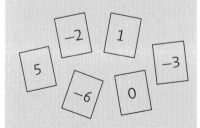

C

21   28   36   45   56   60

Which of the above numbers are multiples of:

43 3

45 7

44 4

46 15?

Find two numbers that are multiples of both:

47 2 and 9   **49** 4 and 7

48 3 and 8   **50** 5 and 6.

Find all the factors of the following numbers.

51 22

55 27

52 28

56 42

53 30

57 40

54 36

58 105

Work out

59 4^2

61 10^2

60 7^2

62 8^2

Copy the sequence. Write the next four terms.

63 33 40 47 54

64 0·1 0·3 0·5 0·7

65 −2 −5 −8 −11

66 99 90 81 72

67 15 30 45 60

68 −10 −8 −6 −4

69 80 72 64 56

70 250 300 350 400

Copy and complete these equivalent fractions.
(You may use the fraction charts on page 18.)

1 $\dfrac{1}{2} = \dfrac{\square}{4}$

5 $\dfrac{2}{5} = \dfrac{\square}{10}$

2 $\dfrac{1}{4} = \dfrac{\square}{8}$

6 $\dfrac{2}{3} = \dfrac{\square}{6}$

3 $\dfrac{1}{2} = \dfrac{\square}{6}$

7 $\dfrac{3}{4} = \dfrac{\square}{8}$

5 $\dfrac{1}{2} = \dfrac{\square}{10}$

8 $\dfrac{4}{5} = \dfrac{\square}{10}$

Place in order, smallest first.

9 $\dfrac{3}{4}, \dfrac{1}{2}, \dfrac{5}{8}$

10 $\dfrac{2}{5}, \dfrac{1}{2}, \dfrac{3}{10}$

Change to mixed numbers.

11 $\dfrac{7}{2}$ **15** $\dfrac{19}{8}$

12 $\dfrac{9}{4}$ **16** $\dfrac{25}{6}$

13 $\dfrac{11}{3}$ **17** $\dfrac{37}{10}$

14 $\dfrac{8}{5}$ **18** $\dfrac{249}{100}$

Change to improper fractions.

19 $2\frac{2}{3}$ **23** $5\frac{3}{8}$

20 $4\frac{3}{4}$ **24** $1\frac{37}{100}$

21 $7\frac{1}{10}$ **25** $6\frac{2}{5}$

22 $3\frac{5}{6}$ **26** $4\frac{7}{9}$

Give the value of the underlined figure.

27 1·9̲2 **31** 2̲5·43

28 16̲·38 **32** 7·1̲9

29 39·2̲7 **33** 53·06̲

30 42·5̲ **34** 18·7̲

35 Write the numbers shown by the arrows as decimal fractions.

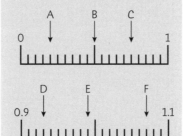

Arrange in order, smallest first.

36 4·72 2·7 4·27 2·47

37 5·91 1·9 1·59 5·19

38 6·8 3·8 3·68 6·38

39 5·7 5·37 5·73 5·3

Round to the nearest:

	metre		pound.
40	3·1 m	**45**	£11·90
41	2·8 m	**46**	£6·20
42	7·3 m	**47**	£29·74
43	4·5 m	**48**	£87·48
44	9·6 m	**49**	£4·50

Write each shaded area as:
a) a fraction
b) a decimal
c) a percentage.

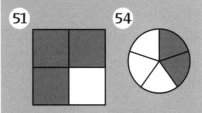
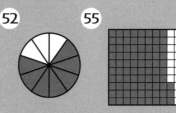

50 **53** **51** **54** **52** **55**

Find

56 $\frac{1}{4}$ of 200 **60** $\frac{1}{6}$ of 30 cm

57 $\frac{3}{4}$ of 200 **61** $\frac{9}{10}$ of 1 m

58 $\frac{1}{10}$ of 240 **62** $\frac{21}{100}$ of £1

59 $\frac{2}{3}$ of 18 **63** $\frac{4}{5}$ of 60p

Find

64 10% of 70

65 25% of 36

66 20% of 80

67 30% of £5·00

68 75% of 60p

69 60% of £2·00

70 50% of £5·50

Copy and complete.

1. $460 + 270 = \square$
2. $55 + 38 = \square$
3. $6 \cdot 3 + \square = 7 \cdot 0$
4. $38 + \square = 100$

5. $\square + 500 = 1247$
6. $\square + 49 = 126$
7. $7 \cdot 9 - 0 \cdot 6 = \square$
8. $117 - 61 = \square$

9. $600 - \square = 514$
10. $8 \cdot 4 - \square = 0 \cdot 8$
11. $\square - 340 = 470$
12. $\square - 57 = 215$

Work out

13. $\begin{array}{r} 438 \\ + 275 \\ \hline \end{array}$

17. $\begin{array}{r} 783 \\ - 139 \\ \hline \end{array}$

14. $\begin{array}{r} 564 \\ + 327 \\ \hline \end{array}$

18. $\begin{array}{r} 548 \\ - 375 \\ \hline \end{array}$

15. $\begin{array}{r} 849 \\ + 286 \\ \hline \end{array}$

19. $\begin{array}{r} 892 \\ - 436 \\ \hline \end{array}$

16. $\begin{array}{r} 774 \\ + 598 \\ \hline \end{array}$

20. $\begin{array}{r} 961 \\ - 728 \\ \hline \end{array}$

Set out correctly and find the totals.

21. $356 + 9 + 1408 + 27$
22. $48 + 3271 + 7 + 685$
23. $£2 \cdot 61 + 92p + £1 \cdot 35$
24. $73p + £5 \cdot 84 + 29p$

Set out correctly and find the differences between:

25. 1957 and 392
26. 63 and 1546
27. £5·38 and £2·94
28. 7·5 and 28·1.

Copy and complete.

29. $14 \times 21 = \square$
30. $32 \times 6 = \square$
31. $0 \cdot 7 \times \square = 2 \cdot 8$
32. $12 \times \square = 0$

33. $\square \times 6 = 54$
34. $\square \times 3 = 1 \cdot 8$
35. $420 \div 7 = \square$
36. $9 \div 1 = \square$

37. $48 \div \square = 6$
38. $150 \div \square = 30$
39. $\square \div 5 = 4 \cdot 0$
40. $\square \div 10 = 3 \cdot 1$

Copy and complete.

41. $\begin{array}{r} 128 \\ \times \quad 6 \\ \hline \end{array}$

43. $\begin{array}{r} 537 \\ \times \quad 8 \\ \hline \end{array}$

42. $\begin{array}{r} 254 \\ \times \quad 9 \\ \hline \end{array}$

44. $\begin{array}{r} 369 \\ \times \quad 7 \\ \hline \end{array}$

Copy and complete.

45. $7 \overline{)114}$
47. $9 \overline{)131}$

46. $6 \overline{)172}$
48. $8 \overline{)278}$

Copy and complete.

49. $\begin{array}{r} 48 \\ \times \quad 17 \\ \hline \\ \hline \end{array}$

50. $\begin{array}{r} 75 \\ \times \quad 36 \\ \hline \\ \hline \end{array}$

Work out

51. $5 \cdot 4 \times 3$
53. $8 \cdot 7 \times 5$
52. $3 \cdot 6 \times 7$
54. $6 \cdot 9 \times 6$

Work out and give the remainder as a fraction.

55. $40 \div 7$
57. $67 \div 9$
56. $263 \div 10$
58. $51 \div 8$

Work out and give the remainder as a decimal.

59. $85 \div 2$
61. $£7 \cdot 20 \div 4$
60. $319 \div 10$
62. $£13 \cdot 00 \div 5$

63. How many seconds are there in one hour?

64. There are 14 sweets in each packet. How many packets can be made from 300 sweets?

65. A school has 243 pupils. 128 are boys. How many girls are there?

66. Sara has 127 marbles. Tina has 39 fewer. How many do they have altogether?

Copy and complete.

1 4·3 km = ☐ m

2 5870 m = ☐ km

3 194 cm = ☐ m

4 2·6 m = ☐ cm

5 0·5 cm = ☐ mm

6 79 mm = ☐ cm

7 3·82 m = ☐ cm

8 7800 m = ☐ km

9 6·25 kg = ☐ g

10 2·3 kg = ☐ g

11 3740 g = ☐ kg

12 500 g = ☐ kg

13 1·4 litres = ☐ ml

14 3·860 litres = ☐ ml

15 2900 ml = ☐ litres

16 480 ml = ☐ litres

Work out the measurement shown by each arrow.

17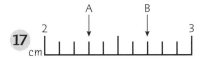

18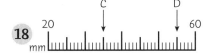

19 **20**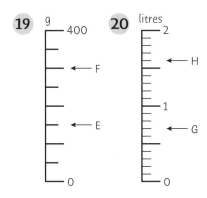

21 A bottle contains 2 litres of cola. Six 200 ml cups are filled from the bottle. How much cola is left?

22 There is 48 cm between the top of a wardrobe and the ceiling. The room has a height of 2·2 metres. How tall is the wardrobe?

23 One tin of peas weighs 300 g. What do fifteen tins weigh in kilograms?

24 A roll of wire is 6 metres long. How many 30 cm lengths can be cut from the roll?

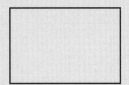

25 What is the area of the rectangle?

26 What is the perimeter of the rectangle?

27 Work out the area and perimeter of these shapes.
   a) rectangle
      6 cm × 4 cm
   b) square 7 cm sides

28 A square field has a perimeter of 400 metres. What is the area of the field?

Copy and complete.

29 36 months = ☐ years

30 2 years = ☐ weeks

31 42 days = ☐ weeks

32 3 days = ☐ hours

33 $6\frac{1}{2}$ hours = ☐ mins.

34 300 seconds = ☐ mins.

35 4 centuries = ☐ years

36 $2\frac{1}{2}$ hours = ☐ mins.

July 1st falls on a Friday. On what day will these dates fall?

37 July 12th

38 July 23rd

39 August 7th

40 June 16th

41 Copy and complete the table showing 12-hour and 24-hour clock times.

12-HOUR CLOCK	24-HOUR CLOCK
4:25 p.m.	
10:30 a.m.	
7:15 p.m.	
	08:42
	21:06
2:55 a.m.	
	11:37
	17:21
7:49 a.m.	
	23:11

Write the names of each of these 2-D shapes.

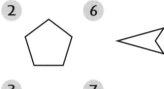

1 **5**

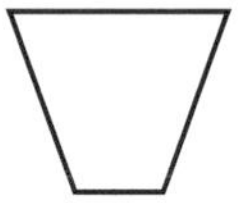

2 **6**

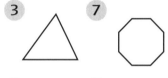

3 **7**

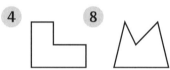

4 **8**

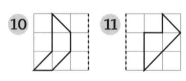

9 Which of the above shapes:
   a) are concave
   b) have parallel lines
   c) are regular?

Use squared paper.
Copy the shape and the mirror line and sketch the reflection.

10 **11**

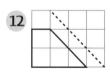

12

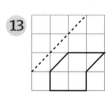

13

For each 3-D shape write:
a) the name of the shape
b) the number of faces
c) the number of edges
d) the number of vertices.

14 **15**

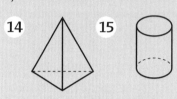

16

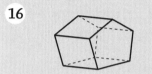

17 **18**

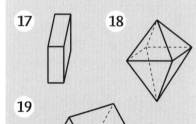

19

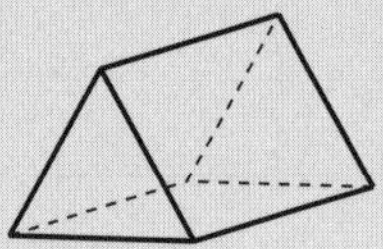

20 **21**

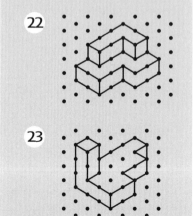

How many cubes are needed to build each shape?

22

23

---

24 Copy the grid.

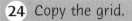

Plot these points and join them up in this order.
(1, 1) (3, 3) (3, 1) (1, 1)

Translate the shape twice.
a) Right 2 squares
b) Up 3 squares

Use a protractor to draw these angles. Write acute or obtuse by each angle.
25 65°   **27** 95°
26 150°   **28** 15°

Calculate the missing angles.

29 **33**

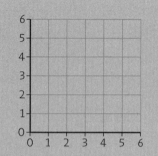
75°   126°

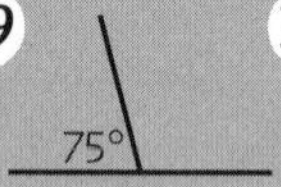

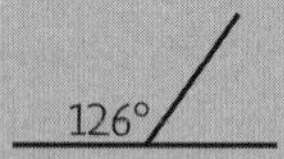

30 **34**

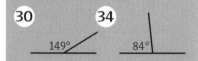
149°   84°

31 **35**

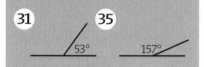
53°   157°

32 **36**

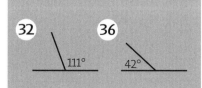
111°   42°

1 This line graph shows the average daily maximum temperature recorded in one week.

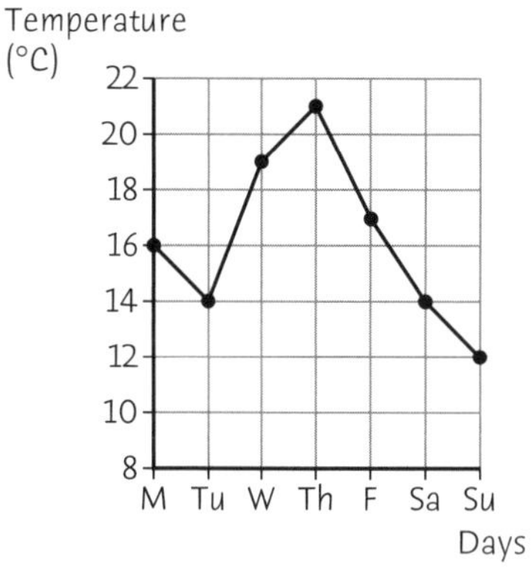

Temperature (°C)

Days

a) What was the range of temperatures?

b) Which day saw the largest rise in temperature?

c) What was the median temperature?

2 Use the table to draw a line graph showing Emma's marks in her weekly tables test.

Week	Mark
1	7
2	9
3	12
4	13
5	15
6	14
7	17
8	17
9	18
10	19

3 This bar chart shows the numbers of children absent in Class 5 in one term.

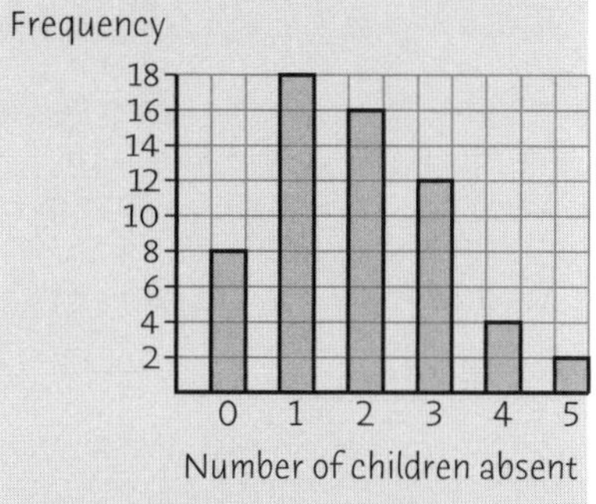

Frequency

Number of children absent

a) What was the largest number of children absent in one day?

b) On how many days were 2 children absent?

c) On how many days were there more than 3 children absent?

d) What was the modal number of children absent?

e) How many days were there in the term?

f) What was the range in the number of children absent?

4 This bar line chart shows the lengths of time spent at a zoo by the visitors on one day.

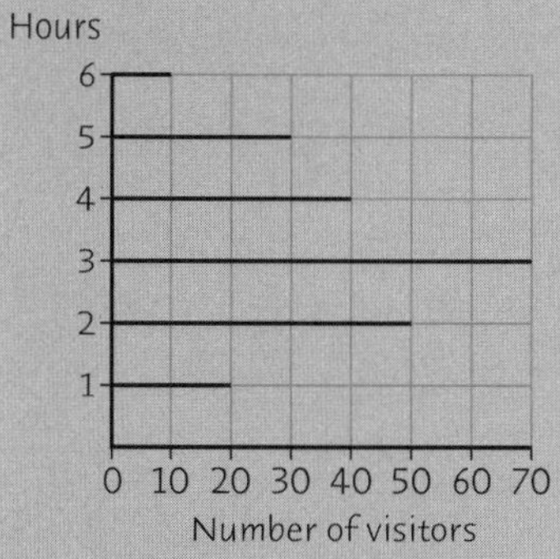

Hours

Number of visitors

a) How many visitors spent four hours at the zoo?

b) What was the longest time spent at the zoo?

c) What was the range in the number of hours spent at the zoo?

d) What was the modal number of hours spent at the zoo?

e) How many people spent less than 3 hours at the zoo?

f) How many people visited the zoo altogether?

TEST 1.

1. Write twenty thousand and seventeen in figures.
2. What is the sum of 84 and 39?
3. Round 3520 to the nearest 1000.
4. Take 0·3 away from 1.
5. Write 172 cm in metres.
6. How many degrees are there in three right-angles?
7. What is the first prime number after 32?
8. Write three quarters as a decimal fraction.
9. What is 450 divided by 9?
10. A film begins at 17:40. It lasts 1 hour 45 minutes. When does it finish?
11. 62 per cent of the children walk to school. What percentage do not walk?
12. What is the area of a square with sides of 20 cm?
13. What is the difference between 800 and 1270?
14. How many 20ps are there in £5?
15. What number is ten times greater than 1·9?
16. The temperature is 7°C. It falls by 10°C. What is the new temperature?
17. Write nine quarters as a mixed number.
18. Multiply 40 by 900.
19. A jug contains 1·5 litres of water. 700 ml is poured out. How much water is left?
20. How many tenths make two fifths?
21. What is seven squared?
22. Double 760.
23. What is one eighth of 72?
24. How many minutes are there in two and a half hours?

TEST 2

1. What is 1·5 less than 3·9?
2. Write three tenths as a percentage.
3. Divide 28 000 by 100.
4. What is half of 94?
5. Write twelve thousand and nine in figures.
6. What is the seventh multiple of 9?
7. Ten tins weigh 4 kg altogether. What is the weight of one tin in grams?
8. What is the total of 183 and 71?
9. A journey begins at 13:25. It finishes at 17:20. How long does it take?
10. What is 50 per cent of 19?
11. Round 12·6 to the nearest whole number.
12. How many eighths make one half?
13. How many degrees is one third of a right-angle?
14. Subtract 240 from 1000.
15. What is the product of 23 and 6?
16. The temperature is −2°C. It rises by 8°C. What is the new temperature?
17. Each book is 8 mm wide. What is the width of 50 books in centimetres?
18. What is 0·2 multiplied by 10?
19. June 19th is a Friday. On what day does July 1st fall?
20. Six pens cost £1·50. What is the cost of one pen?
21. What is 0·29 increased by 0·13?
22. Write $1\frac{5}{7}$ as an improper fraction.
23. What is eight squared?
24. A rectangular field is 120 metres long and 70 metres wide. What is its perimeter?

A

Find a pair of numbers with:

1 a sum of 13 and a product of 36.

2 a sum of 19 and a product of 88.

3 a sum of 15 and a product of 56.

4 a sum of 12 and a product of 36.

5 a sum of 12 and a product of 27.

6 a sum of 29 and a product of 180.

7 a sum of 17 and a product of 42.

8 a sum of 25 and a product of 100.

9 a sum of 15 and a product of 54.

10 a sum of 18 and a product of 45.

B

Find the number.

1 below 40
a prime number
the sum of its digits is 11

2 a square number
a 2-digit number
the sum of its digits is 10

3 a 2-digit number
a prime number
the product of its digits is 12

4 a multiple of 50
a 3-digit number
a multiple of 11

5 a multiple of 7
a 2-digit number
the product of its digits is 30

6 a prime number
a factor of 51
a 2-digit number

7 a multiple of 9
a 2-digit number
the sum of its digits is 18

8 a square number
a 2-digit number
the product of its digits is 8

C

1 Use a calculator.
Find two *consecutive* numbers
with a product of:

a) 121   d) 462   g) 342
b) 182   e) 272   h) 1332
c) 870   f) 1056   i) 1560

2 Use a calculator.
Find a pair of prime numbers with
a product of:

a) 65   d) 119   g) 111
b) 69   e) 533   h) 217
c) 85   f) 473   i) 1769

3 Copy and complete by writing the missing number in the box.

a) $\square + 16 - 7 = 44$

b) $\square - 19 + 12 = 65$

c) $\square + 47 - 21 = 36$

d) $\square \times 6 \div 8 = 9$

e) $\square \times 4 \div 2 = 14$

f) $\square \times 6 \div 10 = 9$

g) $\square \div 3 \times 5 = 100$

h) $\square \div 6 \times 9 = 72$

i) $\square \div 10 \times 6 = 3$

Copy and complete by writing the missing digits in the boxes.

1 4☐ + ☐3 = 109

2 ☐7 + 9☐ = 130

3 5☐ + ☐7 = 85

4 ☐3 + 1☐ = 85

5 5☐ + ☐6 = 95

6 ☐6 + 5☐ = 138

7 6☐ + ☐4 = 143

8 ☐6 + 3☐ = 134

9 4☐ − ☐8 = 8

10 ☐3 − 2☐ = 18

11 19☐ − ☐5 = 119

12 ☐0 − 4☐ = 7

13 9☐ − ☐6 = 36

14 ☐☐7 − 8☐ = 85

15 11☐ − ☐7 = 71

B

Copy and complete by writing the missing digits in the boxes.

1
```
   ☐3☐
 + 1☐2
  ─────
   4 0 8
```

2
```
   4☐4
 − ☐2☐
  ─────
   3 4 5
```

3
```
    ☐7
 ×   2
  ─────
   1 3☐
```

4
```
   3☐8
 + ☐0☐
  ─────
   5 6 3
```

5
```
   ☐1☐
 − 2☐3
  ─────
    6 3
```

6
```
    ☐6
 ×   4
  ─────
   3 4☐
```

7
```
   ☐8☐
 + 1☐8
  ─────
   7 6 1
```

8
```
   6☐1
 − ☐7☐
  ─────
   4 1 3
```

9
```
    ☐7
 ×   6
  ─────
   3 4☐
```

10
```
   3☐9
 + ☐5☐
  ─────
   7 0 5
```

11
```
   ☐8☐
 − 1☐6
  ─────
   4 5 9
```

12
```
    ☐9
 ×   3
  ─────
   1 1☐
```

C

Copy and complete by writing the missing digits in the boxes.

1
```
   ☐2☐
 − 1☐4
  ─────
   1 5 2
```

2
```
   ☐☐7
 ×   3
  ─────
   1 2 8☐
```

3
```
      5 3
   3)1☐9
```

4
```
   2☐5
 − ☐6☐
  ─────
    7 6
```

5
```
   ☐☐9
 ×   6
  ─────
   1 4 3☐
```

6
```
      5 7
   4)2☐8
```

7
```
   ☐3☐
 − 4☐7
  ─────
    7 4
```

8
```
   ☐☐3
 ×   4
  ─────
   2 1 3☐
```

9
```
      9 4
   6)5☐4
```

10
```
   4☐4
 − ☐4☐
  ─────
   2 6 6
```

11
```
   ☐☐4
 ×   7
  ─────
   1 2 8☐
```

12
```
      2 8
   5)1☐0
```

Challenge!